CATALOGING COMPUTER FILES

By Nancy B. Olson

Edited by Edward Swanson

**Published for the
Minnesota AACR 2 Trainers
by
Soldier Creek Press**
Lake Crystal, Minnesota
1992

First edition

ISBN 0-936996-47-1

Library of Congress Cataloging-in-Publication Data

```
Olson, Nancy B.
      Cataloging computer files / by Nancy B. Olson ; edited by Edward Swanson.
         p.    cm. -- (Minnesota AACR 2 Trainers series : no. 2)
      Based on the Anglo-American cataloguing rules, 2nd ed., 1988 revision.
      Rev. ed. of: A manual of AACR 2 examples for microcomputer software with
   MARC tagging and coding.  1988.
      ISBN 0-936996-47-1 : $25.00
      1. Cataloging of computer files--Handbooks, manuals, etc. 2. Anglo-American
   cataloguing rules--Handbooks, manuals, etc.  3. Descriptive cataloging--Rules--
   Handbooks, manuals, etc.  I. Swanson, Edward, 1941-    . II. Olson, Nancy B.
   Manual of AACR 2 examples for microcomputer software with MARC tagging and
   coding.  III. Minnesota AACR 2 Trainers.  IV. Title.  V. Series.
   Z695.47.O47 1992
   025.3'44—dc20                                                      92-28773
                                                                      CIP
```

Soldier Creek Press
P.O. Box 734
Lake Crystal, Minnesota 56055-0734 USA

Nancy B. Olson, President
Edward Swanson, Editor-in-Chief
Sharon Olson, Managing Editor

This book was created electronically using Microsoft Word and Aldus PageMaker on the Apple Macintosh IIfx
computer. Printing and binding by Corporate Graphics International.

CONTENTS

PREFACE

The first edition of this manual was published in 1983, with the title *A Manual of AACR 2 Examples for Microcomputer Software and Video Games*. It included information on the development of cataloging rules, the problems related to using AACR 2 chapter 9 for cataloging microcomputer software, and the process leading up to the development of the *Guidelines for Using AACR 2 Chapter 9 for Cataloging Microcomputer Software* (ALA, 1984). Twenty-five examples were included. Correction sheets were distributed with the manual after the *Guidelines* were developed. It was used in several Minnesota AACR 2 Trainers workshops.

The second edition of the manual was published in 1986 under the title *A Manual of AACR 2 Examples for Microcomputer Software*. This edition followed the *Guidelines*, with comments concerning changes being made to chapter 9 of AACR 2 by the Joint Steering Committee for the Revision of AACR. This manual contained 47 examples, all new to the second edition. It also included, as an appendix, lists of computer-related subject headings compiled by the author from LCSH and its supplements and weekly lists, and a list of LC classification numbers, also compiled by the author, from LC schedules and supplements.

A second edition, revised, was announced but not published.

The third edition contained 18 examples selected from those previously used and those more recently cataloged by the author at Mankato State University. Each example was shown with MARC codes and tags as prepared for OCLC input, as well as in the more familiar catalog card format.

This revision of the third edition follows the *Anglo-American Cataloguing Rules,* second edition, 1988 revision (ALA, 1988). It includes 22 additional examples (for a total of 40), many of which are CD-ROM products.

For those desiring more information on this type of cataloging, and/or more examples, see my book, *Cataloging Microcomputer Software* (Libraries Unlimited, 1988). It includes 100 examples, some coded and tagged for OCLC input. It also includes a history of the development of cataloging rules for computer files and a detailed annotated bibliography of over 100 articles and books on the subject. Lists of computer-related subject headings and classification numbers, both Dewey and LC, also are included, as is a glossary of microcomputer-related terms.

As always, thanks to my daughter-in-law, Sharon Olson, for her patient work with this manuscript and with all the Soldier Creek responsibilities.

— Nancy B. Olson

THE MINNESOTA AACR 2 TRAINERS

One of the problems of implementation of AACR 2 was the need to teach new cataloging rules to all catalogers in the country. The process used in Minnesota is detailed in the following article by Edward Swanson, as reprinted from the *Minitex Messenger* (vol. 6, no. 2, Sept. 1980).

AACR 2 in Minnesota
by Edward Swanson

Planning for AACR 2 in Minnesota began in the winter of 1979 when invitations to nominate persons to attend the Introductory Program on the Anglo-American Cataloguing Rules, Second Edition, Preconference in Dallas in June 1979 were mailed to library associations, state library agencies, and other groups throughout the United States. Those selected to attend the Preconference were to be trained in AACR 2 and then would form the core group of trainers in their home states. The Preconference was planned by the Ad Hoc AACR 2 Introductory Program Committee, established by the ALA Resources and Technical Services Division and chaired by Doralyn Hickey.

Thirteen Minnesotans, nominated by MLA, MEMO, MINITEX, OPLIC, SMILE, CLIC, Mankato State University, the University of Minnesota Libraries and the University of Minnesota Library School, were selected to attend from Minnesota. They included:

Jean Aichele, St. Cloud State University;
Julia Blixrud, MINITEX;
Helen Gbala, College of St. Catherine;
Mary Hanley, University of Minnesota Bio-Medical Library;
Helen Liu, University of Minnesota;
Sue Mahmoodi, OPLIC;
Phyllis Marion, University of Minnesota Law Library;
Barbara N. Moore, Mankato State University;
Tom Nichol, St. John's University;
Nancy B. Olson, Mankato State University;
Irene Schilling, Augsburg College;
Wesley Simonton, University of Minnesota Library School;
Jan Snesrud, University of Minnesota.

Marilyn H. Jones, University of Minnesota, and Edward Swanson, Minnesota Historical Society, who were members of the Introductory Program Committee, served as trainers at the Preconference.

The Preconference began with four videotapes dealing with the history of code revison, description, choice of access points, and form of headings. Small group sessions dealt in depth with description, choice, and form. The final programs at the Preconference dealt with workshop planning and effective communication in a small group setting.

The 15 Minnesotans, soon to become known as the Minnesota AACR 2 Trainers, began meeting in July to plan the training sessions in Minnesota.

The first program was held in October at the U of M St. Paul Campus. "Planning for AACR 2" began with a description of the major changes in AACR 2, given by Wesley Simonton. Nancy Olson discussed the Library of Congress's decisions about adopting the code, Tom Nichol related decisions made by OCLC, and Phyllis Marion presented options a library can adopt in relating entries in its catalogs created under AACR 2 and under earlier codes. A panel composed of Walt Dunlap, Arrowhead Library System; Sanford Berman, Hennepin County Library; Barbara N. Moore; and Helen Liu described options for various types and sizes of libraries in coping with the changes.

At the November 1979 meeting of the Minnesota Library Association, Frances Hinton, head of the processing department at the Free Library of Philadelphia, spoke on changes to forms of headings that will occur after the adoption of AACR 2. Hinton was a member of the ALA Catalog Code Revision Committee and deputy ALA representative to the Joint Steering Committee. She is now the ALA representative to the reconstituted Joint Steering Committee and its chair.

The Trainers spent the winter months preparing for the first series of workshops, held in April and May at six locations around the state. These workshops dealt with changes in descriptions, choice of entry, and form of headings under AACR 2. The Trainers divided into three groups, each group covering one of these topics. In addition to planning the sessions to be given on the particular topic, each group also assembled cataloging examples and copy that were compiled into a publication, *A Manual of AACR 2 Examples*. This manual was distributed to each workshop attendee as the basic text for the workshop sessions. In addition, it has been made available for sale and some 1,500 copies have been sold thus far throughout the United States and Canada and to libraries in such places as Iceland, Singapore, and Malaysia. The manual has received favorable reviews from various sources and has been adopted as a textbook in several library education programs.

The first workshop was held April 11, 1980, at the Hennepin County Southdale Library followed by ones at Bethany College, Winona State University, St. John's University, Bemidji State University, and the University of Minnesota, Duluth. Almost 200 librarians from all types of libraries in Minnesota attended these sessions. At each one the three major topics were covered, each taught by one or more members of the group that had worked on that topic. The workshops' reception was probably best exemplified by the remark made by a librarian who had quite a few years of cataloging experience, "I'm not afraid of it any more."

The Technical Services Section of the Minnesota Library Association sponsored a talk by Elizabeth L. Tate at its spring meeting in St. Cloud on the strategies for searching library catalogs using AACR 2 as compared with earlier cataloging codes. Formerly head of the descriptive cataloging division at the Library of Congress, Tate is the editor of *Library Resources & Technical Services*. Also at that meeting, the Minnesota Library Association honored the Minnesota AACR 2 Trainers by presenting them certificates of merit "in recognition of your contribution to the profession by giving your time, energy, and enthusiasm in promoting and teaching AACR 2 to librarians throughout Minnesota."

During the summer of 1980 the Trainers continued their work preparing for a series of workshops on cataloging of specialized types of materials. These workshops, to be held at the Sheraton Inn-Northwest in Minneapolis, Oct. 23-25, will include sessions on cataloging graphics and non-music sound recordings, serials, manuscripts, legal materials, liturgical works and sacred scriptures, early printed books, motion pictures and videorecordings, music scores and music sound recordings, cartographic materials, and three-dimensional artefacts and realia. A repeat of the spring workshops will also be offered, as well as a workshop on cataloging using the Level 1 form of description. Several of these sessions will be repeated during the three days to enable attendees to cover several topics in a short period of time.

On Thursday evening, Oct. 23, there will be a session designed for public services librarians that will cover the basic changes in AACR 2 from earlier cataloging codes. Announcements of the workshops have been mailed to libraries throughout Minnesota, as well as to members of the various library associations in the state.

Minneapolis was the site in August of one of a series of workshops on AACR 2 presented by the Library of Congress. These "LC roadshows" are being held throughout the United States, sponsored by the ALA Resources and Technical Services Division. Six senior members of the cataloging divisions at LC are at each roadshow to describe how the Library of Congress is going to apply AACR 2. Over 200 librarians from the Upper Midwest and Canada attended the Minneapolis session.

Minnesota will be well prepared for Jan. 1, 1981, the "Day-1" for AACR 2. Unlike 1967, when the first edition was adopted (or rather partially adopted) with almost no introduction, a concerted effort has been made to acquaint librairans in the state with the changes that will begin appearing in their catalogs in 1981. This would not have been possible without the Minnesota AACR 2 Trainers. These 15 people took their charge seriously and returned from the Introductory Program Preconference in Dallas ready and willing to work together to carry it out. Interestingly, this work has been carried out without any outside sponsorship or financial support. The group has worked well together, although at times the discussions over what a particular rule means did become somewhat protracted and not a little heated. The key is that the group has been able to work as a group dedicated to a single goal. And best of all, we've had fun doing it!

The October 1980 workshops mentioned in the article above were extremely successful with 200 librarians from five states registered. These workshops were repeated in October 1985 with over 100 attendees. Some of the Trainers were invited to present workshops in other states during this time.

The Trainers organized themselves to present these workshops because they were concerned. There is no state library in Minnesota, nor is there one library association to which all librarians belong. The Trainers could present workshops reaching school, public, academic, and special librarians all at the same time without regard to geographic or political boundaries. By cooperating and sharing their expertise they could present a range of workshops.

The original group of Trainers are listed above. Two of the group, Jean Aichele and Irene Schilling, are now deceased. Several others have retired, and some have left librarianship for other careers. Some have moved into administration.

The Trainers received no funds from any agency, nor did they receive any grant money to support their work. All Trainers volunteered their time (vacation time for most) and received neither pay nor honoraria for their participation in these workshops. Relatively small fees were charged participants in the workshops. Worldwide sales of the basic manual, *A Manual of AACR 2 Examples*, subsidized the workshops and the expenses of the Trainers.

The basic manual was published by Soldier Creek Press. All money received from sales of the first two editions, less actual expenses, was used to finance activities of the Minnesota AACR 2 Trainers.

CATALOGING COMPUTER FILES

CATALOGING COMPUTER FILES

Introduction

Computer files are cataloged by the rules of chapter 9 of the *Anglo-American Cataloguing Rules*, second edition, 1988 revision (ALA, 1988) (AACR 2). The term "computer file" covers all computer software for all types of computers, as well as data files of all types. Both published and unpublished computer files may be cataloged, as may files available only by remote access, including those on local networks, and electronic media available through the Internet and elsewhere.

Because this manual is designed to be used with AACR 2 itself, the text of the rules is not included here.

Scope

The term "computer file" covers all computer software for all types of computers as well as data files of all types. Both published and unpublished computer files may be cataloged. Files available only by remote access may also be cataloged.

Programs in ROM or firmware are considered to be part of the device in which they reside and are described as such. They are not cataloged separately.

Chief Source of Information

Rule 9.0B1 for the chief source of information for computer files directs us to use the title screen or screens for information for cataloging.

If there is no title screen, the information is to be taken from "other formally presented internal evidence" such as menus, program statements, etc.

If the information is not available from the title screen(s) or other internal sources, the following hierarchy is to be used for the chief source of information:

the physical carrier or its labels;
documentation or accompanying material; or
the container.

"Not available" above includes those cases where the cataloger does not have access to equipment needed to run the computer file, as well as those cases for which there is no title screen or screens or other information when the computer file is run.

If the item being cataloged consists of two or more separate physical parts, and a collective title appears on the container but not on the title screens, the container is treated as the chief source of information.

Prescribed Sources of Information

Rule 9.0B2 lists the prescribed sources of information for each area of the bibliographic record.

The title and statement of responsibility area; edition area; publication, distribution, etc., area; and series area are to be taken from the chief source of information, the carrier or its labels, information issued by the publisher, creator, etc., and/or the container. The file characteristics area, physical description area, notes, and standard number and terms of availability area are to be taken from any source.

Information taken for an area from outside the prescribed source for that area is to be enclosed in square brackets.

Title Screens

Title screens are reproduced in this manual for all examples. Most examples are Apple or Macintosh software because these materials were readily available to me.

Apple software usually has title screens with information similar to book title pages or to motion picture title screens. These title screens appear as the item is run. Sometimes credits appear only at the end of a program.

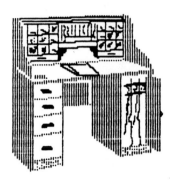

```
I N F O R M A T I O N   M A S T E R ™
By: James A Cox  and  Stephen M Williams
```

```
© COPYRIGHT 1979
James A Cox & High Technology, Inc.
```

Figure 1. Apple software title screen

IBM software does not often display this type of title screen, but may have something similar.

```
Press Esc for no backup, F9 to make backup copy "STORY.&"
IHHHHHHHHHHHHHHHHHHHHHHHHHHHHHHHHHHHHHHHHHHHHHHHHHHHHHHHHHHHHHHHHHHHHHHHHH;
:    PC-Write (R). Version 2.71. Released on 24-Dec-86. Registration #850067
:    (C) Copyright 1983-1986 by Bob Wallace, Quicksoft. All Rights Reserved.   :
:    Shareware: Please help distribute PC-Write by sharing unmodified copies   :
:    of the diskettes in the U.S. and Canada. Please don t copy the manual.    :
:    Please don't share copies elsewhere, to support our foreign publishers.   :
LHHH> If you are using PC-Write, please buy a manual or a registered copy. <HH9
: ZDDDDDDDDDDDDDDDDDDDDDDDDDDDDDDDDDDDDDDDDDDDDDDDDDDDDDDDDDDDDDDDDDDDDD? :
: 3 Compliments of: Quicksoft [this box available for your own message]  3 :
: @DDDDDDDDDDDDDDDDDDDDDDDDDDDDDDDDDDDDDDDDDDDDDDDDDDDDDDDDDDDDDDDDDDDDDDY :
: ZDDDDDDDDDDDDDDDDDDDDDDDDDDDDDDDDDDDDDDDDDDDDDDDDDDDDDDDDDDDDDDDDDDDDDDD? :
: 3 A registered copy provides you all the following benefits for only $89: 3 :
: 3 > Printed hardbound copy of the full PC-Write manual and Quick Guide. 3 :
: 3 > Current PC-Write diskette pair and your unique registration number. 3 :
: 3 > PC-Write support service for one year:  includes telephone support, 3 :
: 3    our quarterly newsletter, and two free update or source diskettes. 3 :
: 3 > A $25 commission when someone registers and gives your reg. number. 3 :
: 3 > Sincere thanks; your support helps us continue to improve PC-Write! 3 :
: @DDDDDDDDDDDDDDDDDDDDDDDDDDDDDDDDDDDDDDDDDDDDDDDDDDDDDDDDDDDDDDDDDDDDDDY :
:    Hardbound manual $45, diskette pair $16. Quantity prices. Group license.  :
:    When you register, give registration #number above, to credit its owner.  :
:    PO, COD, Rush: add $5. Overseas add $20. WA orders add 7.9%. Visa/MC ok.  :
:    Quicksoft, Inc.  206/282-0452.  219 First North #224, Seattle, WA 98109.  :
HHHHHHHHHHHHHHHHHHHHHHHHHHHHHHHHHHHHHHHHHHHHHHHHHHHHHHHHHHHHHHHHHHHHHHHHHHH<
```

Figure 2. IBM title screen

Macintosh software usually does not display a title screen immediately. One must request the information as shown in the following illustration. One "pulls down" this display until the "about" command appears, then "clicks" on the "about" entry. If there is no "about" command, there may be information on some other screen.

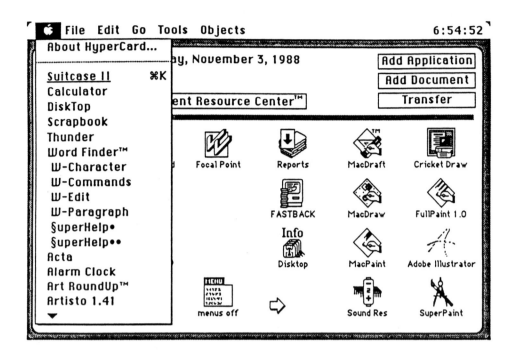

Figure 3. Macintosh "about" screen

4

A title screen appears in the middle of the Macintosh display when the "about" screen is requested.

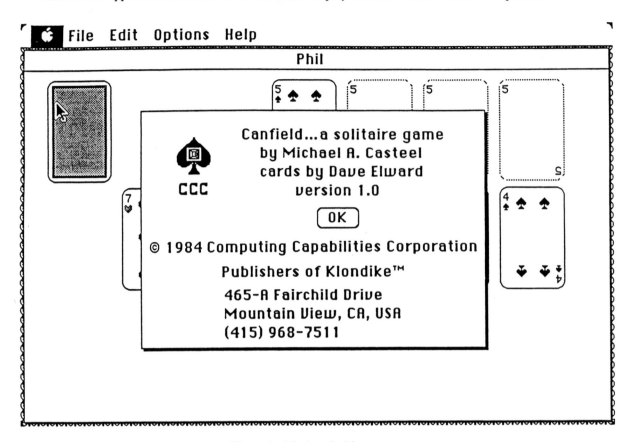

Figure 4. Macintosh title screen

Compact disks may display title and credits screens, or they may not. One I previewed indicated a file named "credits". It included the title frame and all credits I needed! Very useful.

Area 1
Title and Statement of Responsibility Area

9.1B1. Title proper

Record the title proper as instructed in rule 1.1B and the Library of Congress rule interpretations (LCRIs) related to rule 1.1B. The LCRIs appear quarterly in the Library of Congress *Cataloging Service Bulletin* (CSB).

```
About cows
MacDraw
Krell's logo
```
   (The word following the possessive is not to be capitalized according to LCRI A.4A, CSB 31)
```
Parrot Software presents Select
```
   ("Presents" information appearing before the "title" may be ignored only when cataloging motion pictures and videorecordings, according to LCRI 7.1B in CSB 13. It may not be ignored for any other media).

The source of the title proper always is recorded in a note.

9.1C. General Material Designation

The general material designation (GMD) for this material is "computer file." The GMD is to be added immediately following the title proper and is not capitalized.

```
HyperCard stacks [computer file]
1987 economic censuses [computer file]
[Music programs] [computer file]
```

9.1D. Parallel titles

Record parallel titles as instructed in rule 1.1D and the related LCRIs.

```
Préparation à la lecture et à l'addition [GMD] = Getting ready to
read and add
```

9.1E. Other title information

Record other title information as instructed in rule 1.1E and the related LCRIs.

```
Bookends extended [GMD] : the reference management system
```

9.1F. Statements of responsibility

Record statements of responsibility relating to those persons or bodies responsible for the content of the file as instructed in rule 1.1F and the related LCRIs. Sometimes one doesn't know the exact function of a person named on the chief source. As with other types of material, one may transcribe information that appears to be a statement of responsibility into this part of area 1. Responsibility information that appears elsewhere on the item (outside the chief source) that is included in area 1 must be enclosed in square brackets.

6

There may not be any statement of responsibility given in the chief source of information. It is not necessary to have a statement of responsibility. Remember, one is transcribing information appearing prominently in the chief source of information into this area of the bibliographic record. If no person or body is named prominently, no statement of responsibility will be included.

```
Catlab [GMD] : a genetics simulation / J.F. Kinnear
Desert storm [GMD] : the war in the Persian Gulf / a product of
Warner New Media in association with Time magazine
```

Give statements relating to collaborators, sponsors, etc., or to persons or bodies who have prepared or contributed to the production of the file, in a note.

Area 2
Edition Area

9.2B. Edition statement

Any indication that the item in hand differs somehow from a previous appearance of the same item suggests the presence of an edition. The concept of edition is treated very broadly in this chapter of AACR 2. Transcribe a statement relating to a named reissue of a computer file, or to an edition of the file that contains differences from other editions, as instructed in rule 1.2B and the related LCRIs. Words indicating an edition statement include *edition, issue, version, release, level,* and *update.*

```
HyperCard stacks [GMD] / Educorp. -- Version 3.0
Verbum interactive [GMD]. -- Macintosh ed.
dBASE II [GMD]. -- Ver[sion] 2.41A
    (Missing letters are added in brackets for clarity)
Omnis 3 database manager [GMD]. -- Version number 3.10. MAC
```

One must be careful when cataloging computer software to differentiate between a new version of the software and the version of the operating system needed to run that software. Both may be expressed as "version 3.3" or some other decimal number. The term that refers to the operating system may include the letters "DOS" or "CP/M" or some combination of numbers and letters, frequently including the letters "OS" for "operating system." A statement referring to the version of the software is recorded as an edition statement; a statement referring to the version of the operating system needed to run that software may be included in the system requirements note.

Area 3
File Characteristics Area

9.3B. File characteristics

The file characteristics area is made up of two parts. The type of file is designated in the first part of area 3, in which the following terms may be used:

```
Computer data
Computer program(s)
Computer data and program(s)
```

The word "computer" in the above terms is optional if GMDs are used.

Additional information may be added to the above terms if the information is readily available. For data, one may add the number or approximate number of records and/or bytes:

```
Computer data (5 files)
Computer data (3743 records)
Computer data (2 files : 400, 500 records)
Computer data (1 file : 1500 bytes)
Computer data (1 file : 434 records, 1672 bytes)
```

For programs, one may add the number or approximate number of statements and/or bytes:

```
Computer program (1 file : 684 statements)
Computer program (43 statements)
Computer programs (4 files : 300, 450, 200, 125 bytes)
```

Combinations of this information may be used for computer data and programs cataloged together.

The Library of Congress has decided not to use area 3 unless it provides information not available elsewhere in the bibliographic record.

Area 4
Publication, Distribution, etc., Area

9.4C. Place of publication, distribution, etc.

Record the place of publication, distribution, etc., as instructed in rule 1.4C and the related LCRIs.

```
Grand Rapids, MN
Santa Monica, Calif.
[United States]
```

The two-letter postal abbreviation for a state name is not to be used unless it appears on the item. If the state name appears in full, it is to be abbreviated as shown in Appendix B of AACR 2. "United States" is not abbreviated in this area of the bibliographic record.

9.4D. Name of publisher, distributor, etc.

Record the name of the publisher, distributor, etc. as instructed in rule 1.4D and the related LCRIs.

```
Oak Park, Mich. : Sensible Software
Bellevue, WA : Temporal Acuity Products ; Owatonna, MN : Distrib-
uted exclusively by Musitronic
```

9.4F. Date of publication, distribution, etc.

Record the date of publication, distribution, etc., as instructed in rule 1.4F and the related LCRIs.

```
San Mateo, CA : Blyth Software, c1985
McLean, VA : Decision Support Software, [198-]
Bethesda, MD : Disclosure, 1990-
[United States] : Reactur, 1991
1985
```

On the disk label shown below, two copyright dates are given. The one preceded by "DOS 3.3" is the copyright date of the operating system, not of the computer file on the disk.

McGraw-Hill/Courseware® Authoring System

SIDE 2   **DEMONSTRATION DISKETTE**

Copyright © 1984 by McGraw-Hill, Inc. All rights reserved. Manufactured in the United States of America. Use of this software is subject to the restrictions contained in the appropriate McGraw-Hill Software Licence Agreement.

DOS 3.3 Copyright © Apple, 1980, 1981   ISBN 0-07-810032-1

Figure 6. Disk label with DOS copyright date, software copyright date

Area 5
Physical Description Area

Do **not** give a physical description for a computer file that is available only by remote access. This is the only type of material for which there is no area 5. One does not give a physical description when there is no physical item to describe. Explain in a note how to access the file.

9.5B. Extent of item

Record the number of physical units of the item being described by giving the number of parts in arabic numerals and one of the following terms as appropriate:

```
computer cartridge
computer cassette
computer disk
computer reel
```

Notice "disk" is spelled with a "k."

One may choose to be more specific:

```
computer chip cartridge
computer tape cartridge
computer tape reel
computer laser optical disk
```

We ignore the plastic/paper "sleeve" in which the 5¼ inch disk is enclosed. We also ignore the permanent plastic case on the Macintosh disk, and give the diameter of the disk inside that case. Similar non-removable cases for other size or types of disks are also ignored.

As new materials become available, one may choose to use the specific name of the physical carrier, preferably qualified by the word "computer."

CD-ROM disks

I have chosen to use "computer disk" for the extent of item, rather than the more specific (and lengthier) "computer laser optical disk." The same technology, when used for recording music and cataloged by rules of AACR 2 chapter 6, is called "sound disc"; when used for film and cataloged by AACR 2 chapter 7, it is called "videodisc."

The area 5 combination of "computer disk" and size of 4¾ inches should tell the user what it is. The system requirements note specifying a CD-ROM drive reinforces this.

9.5C. Other physical details

If the file is encoded to produce sound, give the abbreviation "sd." If the file is encoded to display in two or more colors, give the abbreviation "col."

```
1 computer disk : sd., col.
1 computer cartridge : col.
2 computer cassettes : sd.
```

Optionally, give information on number of sides used, recording density, and sectoring, if the information is readily available and if it is considered to be important to the cataloging agency.

9.5D. Dimensions

Give dimensions of the physical carrier as follows:

Disks. Give the diameter of the disk in inches, rounded to the next ¼ inch up.

```
1 computer disk : sd., col. ; 5 1/4 in.
```

Cartridges. Give, in inches rounded to the next ¼ inch up, the length of the side of the cartridge that is to be inserted into the machine.

```
1 computer cartridge : col. ; 3 1/2 in.
```

Cassettes. Give the length and height of the face of the cassette in inches, rounded to the next ⅛ inch up.

```
1 computer cassette ; 1 1/8 x 2 3/8 in.
```

For packages containing disks of different sizes, give the total number of disks and the range of sizes.

```
5 computer disks : sd., col. ; 3 1/2-5 1/4 in.
```

For packages including backup disks, include the backup disk(s) in the extent of item and make a note about them:

```
Second disk is backup
Three disks are backup copy
```

If any of the disks is considered to be accompanying material, it may be listed in that part of area 5.

9.5E. Accompanying material

Record the details of accompanying material as instructed in rule 1.5E and the related LCRIs.

```
1 computer disk : sd., col. ; 5 1/4 in. + 1 user's manual
1 computer disk ; 3 1/2 in. + 1 set of notes for the teacher + 20
identical sets of student notes
2 computer disks : col. ; 3 1/2 in. + 1 v. (446 p. : ill. ; 28 cm.)
1 computer disk : sd., col. ; 4 3/4 in. + 1 user's guide + 2 computer
disks (3 1/2 in.)
```

Area 6
Series Area

9.6B. Series statements

Record every series statement as instructed in rule 1.6 and the related LCRIs.

```
Mathematics series
Computer learning games
IBM PC apprentice personal computer learning series
```

Area 7
Note Area

Notes contain useful information that cannot be fitted into other areas of the description. Give notes in the order in which they are listed here. When appropriate, combine two or more notes to make one note as permitted by rule 1.7A5.

Remember, information must be given somewhere in the bibliographic record if an added entry is to be included for that information.

9.7B1a. Nature and scope

Make notes on the nature or scope of the file unless it is apparent from the rest of the description.

```
Word processing program
Fantasy/adventure game
Simulation game
"A software development and documentation package for the Apple II"--
Manual
```
(A quoted note cites the source as shown, unless the information is taken from the chief source of information)
```
Interactive media
```

9.7B1b. System requirements

Always make a note on the system requirements of the file. The note is preceeded by "System requirements:" and the characteristics, if known, are given in the following order, with each preceded by a semicolon that does not have a space before it.

make and model of the computer(s) on which the file is designed to run;
amount of memory required;
name of the operating system;
software requirements including the programming language;
kind and characteristics of any required or recommended peripherals

The cataloger should not list items of equipment that are part of the standard computer system, such as disk drives, monitor, or cables.

```
System requirements: Apple IIe; 128K; ProDOS; 2 disk drives; printer
System requirements: IBM PC; 132 column printer
System requirements: Macintosh II or greater; 4 MB RAM; CD-ROM drive
```

9.7B1c. Mode of access

If the file is available only by remote access, always specify the mode of access.

```
Online access via DIALOG
Locally available through Corvus system
Available through the Internet
```

9.7B2. Language and script

Give an indication of the language and/or script of the spoken or written content of the file unless this is apparent from the rest of the description.

```
Text on screen in French and English; manual in English
```

This note is not to be used for programming language.

9.7B3. Source of title proper

A note *must* be made giving the source of the title proper.

```
Title from title screen
Title from disk label
Title from manual
Title from container
Title supplied by cataloger
```

9.7B4. Variations in title

Give other titles found on the item or its accompanying documentation if the variation from the title proper is significant.

```
Title on guide: Personal finance system
```
    (Title proper: Dynacomp finance)
```
Title on teacher's guide: Regions of the United States
```
    (Title proper: Regions)
```
Also called: Missing math facts
```
    (Title proper: Missing facts)

9.7B5. Parallel titles and other title information

Give parallel titles and other title information not recorded in the title and statement of responsibility area if they are considered to be important.

```
Title on manual: Bookends, the reference management system
```
    (Title proper: Bookends)
```
Subtitle on manual: Dot addressable graphics
```
    (Title proper: OkigraphII)

9.7B6. Statements of responsibility

Give statements of responsibility not recorded in the title and statement of responsibility area, if the information is considered important.

```
Program author, Bessie Chin ; manual authors, Tracy Deliman and Chris
Doerr
```
    (Information is not from chief source, so it is not necessarily recorded in area 1; if recorded in
    area 1 it would be enclosed in square brackets)
```
Created by Howard Berenbom
```

Sometimes the person or body responsible for the content of the program is named only in the copyright statement. In that case, the information from the copyright statement may be transcribed in a note.

```
Copyright by Richard Bruce Rickard
Copyright by Optical Media International
```

Statements relating to collaborators and/or sponsors may be given here. Persons or bodies who have prepared or contributed to the production of the item may be named here if they are not named elsewhere in the description and if the information is considered important.

9.7B7. Edition and history

Make notes relating to the edition being described or to the history of an item.

```
    Based on: About cows / by Sara Rath. Ashland, WI : Heartland Press,
c1987.
```

9.7B8. File characteristics

Give important file characteristics that have not been included in the file characteristics area.

```
    File updated at irregular intervals
    File size: 73,251 bytes (12 Aug. 1991)
```

9.7B9. Publication, distribution, etc.

Make notes on publication, distribution, etc., details that are not included in area 4 but that are considered to be important.

```
    Manual published: Wentworth, N.H. : COMPress, 1985
        (Package distributed by Conduit)
```

9.7B10. Physical description

Give important physical details that cannot be included in the physical description area.
For a file available by remote access, give here any physical details (e.g., color, sound) if the information is readily available and is considered important.

```
    Second disk is back-up
    Stereo.
    Graphs displayed in red, yellow, and blue
    In two binders
    One disk contains word processing program, the other the dictionary
for the spellcheck program
```

9.7B11. Accompanying material

Give details of accompanying material not already mentioned.

```
    Booklet contains program listings for all games on the disk
    Manual includes tutorial
    Teacher's guide includes reproducible activity masters with answer
key
    IBM PC disks for installing the system
```

9.7B12. Series

Make notes on series data that cannot be given in the series area.

```
    Series title on some disks: Language arts series
```

9.7B13. Dissertations

If the file is a dissertation, make a note as instructed in rule 1.7B13.

```
Thesis (M.S.)--Mankato State University, 1984
```

9.7B14. Audience

Make a brief note of the intended audience for, or the intellectual level of, a file if this information is stated in or on the item, its container, or accompanying material.

```
Intended audience: Grade range, 7-12; reading level 7
For use only by law enforcement personnel
    (A restriction made by the publisher)
```

9.7B16. Other formats

Make notes on other formats in which the file has been issued, if that information is available.

```
Data issued also in printed form
Issued also for IBM PC
```

9.7B17. Summary

Give a brief objective summary of the purpose and content of the item unless another part of the description gives enough information.

```
Summary: Arithmetic games for use by individual students in grades 2-6
Summary: Simulation game on wildlife management for use by groups of
students in grades 6-12; takes ca. 20 min. to run
Summary: Spelling tutorials for individual students in grades 2-8
with 16 levels within each of three groups (grades 2-4, 5-6, 7-8). Eight
lessons per level
Summary: Teacher's grade book program that can keep up to 32 grades
per six-week period for as many as six periods and 40 students per class
Summary: Correspondents' reports, eyewitness accounts, photos, audio
recordings, maps, charts, research, and key documents gathered by the
editorial staff of Time
```

9.7B18. Contents

Make a list of the parts of a file.

```
Contents: ABC time -- Spelling zoo -- Letter game
Contents: pt. 1. Arthropoda -- pt. 2. Mollusca
```

Make notes on partial contents when appropriate.

```
Second disk contains portions of the CIJE ERIC data base
```

If desired, one may combine summary information with the contents, bracketing the supplied information.

```
Contents: Fish [simulation on blood circulation] -- Minerals
[identification guide for 29 minerals] -- Odell Lake [simulation
involving foodweb of fish] -- Quakes [simulation in locating epicenter
of earthquake] -- Ursa [tutorial on constellations]
```

9.7B19. Numbers borne by the item

Give important numbers borne by the item other than ISBNs and ISSNs. If transcribed exactly from the item, give these numbers in quotation marks.

```
Control number B-187
```

9.7B20. Copy being described, library's holdings, and local restrictions on use

Make notes on any peculiarities and imperfections of the item being described that are considered to be important. These are local notes; all other notes are general.

```
ERC has only no. 3
For use only by med tech classes
```

9.7B21. "With" notes

If the description is of a separately titled part of an item lacking a collective title, make a note beginning "With:" and listing the other separately title parts of the item in the order in which they appear there.

```
With: HyperCard.
```

Area 8
Standard Number and Terms of Availability Area

9.8B. Standard number

There is no standard number for computer files, although the publisher may have used an ISBN anyway. Record any ISBN or ISSN found on the item or on accompanying material.

```
ISBN 0-936996-34-x (manual)
```

Access Points

Main Entry

Main entries are chosen on the basis of the rules in chapter 21, just as is done for books. Packages of computer software may have main entry under the heading for a person. The rules define a personal author as the one "chiefly responsible for the creation of the intellectual or artistic content of a work" (21.1A1). It will be rare for computer files to have main entry under the heading for a corporate body, because rule 21.1B2 restricts main entry under a corporate body to works "of an administrative nature dealing with the corporate body itself," some legal and governmental works, works recording the "collective thought of the body," and works resulting from the "collective activity of a performing group as a whole." Those items not entered under a personal or corporate body heading are entered under title.

Person named in copyright statements

Early commercial computer software, in the 16K, 32K, 48K, 64K, and 128K days, often was the product of one or two persons who designed and wrote the program and any accompanying material. These programs were given main entry under the heading for the person. The complex programs of today generally are the product of teams of people working for large software firms. Main entry for these is almost always under title.

Information contained in the copyright statement may be considered when determining the main entry. For some packages of computer software, a person is named only in the copyright statement. If there is no accompanying written material, and no name given as author in the chief source of information, but a person is named in the copyright statement, the information is not to be transcribed in the statement of responsibility, but is given in a note

```
    Copyright by Howard Bloem
```

and the person named may be considered when choosing main entry. The person named in the copyright statement may be considered to be chiefly responsible for the creation of the intellectual content of the work may be chosen for the main entry heading.

If, however, a manual or other written material is included in the package, one must consider the authorship of the written material as well as the authorship of the program itself. If the written material is by the same person, the copyright holder, that person is clearly responsible for the creation of the entire work. If the written material is by a different person, I would consider responsibility "diffuse" (21.1C), and would use title main entry.

Form of entry

The form of heading for personal names is determined from the rules in AACR 2 chapter 22, for corporate bodies from those in chapter 24. The LC authority file should always be searched to see if a heading has been established.

Added Entries

Added entries are determined according to rules 21.29-21.30. I recommend making an entry (main or added) for every person named prominently and for most, if not all, of the corporate bodies involved. I also recommend making title added entries for any variant forms of title that would file differently in the catalog for which you are cataloging. The item titled

```
    Mathematics.  Volume 2, Beginning addition
```

should have a title added entry made for the title "Beginning addition."

Those using the MARC format through one of the bibliographic utilities or a local network may make an added entry for the make and model of computer, using field 753. This added entry may be considered to fall within the scope of rule 21.29D.

SUBJECT ACCESS

Subject access includes both subject headings and classification numbers, those subject-related bits of information that provide access to the subject content of the work. Subject access is not covered by the rules for descriptive cataloging. There are no rules for subject access; a library is free to choose the type and amount of subject access needed for its patrons.

Subject Headings

The *Library of Congress Subject Headings* (LCSH) and the *Sears List of Subject Headings* are the two types most commonly used in the United States. LCSH is used by most academic libraries, as well as by many public libraries and special libraries. Sears headings are used by many school and smaller public libraries.

LCSH now is issued annually. Subject headings for all examples in this manual have been taken from the 14th edition (Library of Congress, 1991).

Guidelines on Subject Access to Microcomputer Software was published by ALA in 1986. These guidelines recommend "that headings be assigned for the topic or genre of the software" (p. 5).

Subject headings should reflect what an item is about, rather than the form in which the information is presented. However, genre headings such as **Fantasy games; Electronic spreadsheets** may be used as appropriate.

Form subdivisions

If a form subdivision is desired, LC has established the following two subject subdivisions:

—Software
—Juvenile software

Type of computer, etc.

It is desirable to provide access to the type of computer needed to operate the software. It also may be desirable to provide access to the programming language used and the operating system needed. This information is all given in the system requirements note (MARC field 538) and may be accessed through MARC field 753. The ALA *Guidelines* state "The committee recommends that [subject] headings *not be assigned* for the name of the program, the name of the computer, the computer language, the operating system, or any other information described in the system requirements note." (p. 5)

If we have software that runs on an Apple computer and make a subject heading for that computer, we are mixing works about the use of the Apple computer with works that run on an Apple. We can provide subject access for the topic of the software, and for the genre involved, but should not make subject headings for the physical characteristics.

It has been argued that added entries for that information are not appropriate according to AACR 2. However, rule 21.29D states "If, in the context of a given catalogue, an added entry is required under a heading or title other than those prescribed in 21.30, make it." Subject headings for this information about make and model of computer, programming language, and operating system are not appropriate, as the computer file is not *about* those topics. If we want to provide access to that information for our users, an added entry is our only other option.

Classification

As with subject headings, classification should reflect the content of the material being cataloged rather than its format.

Classification numbers may be chosen from the Library of Congress classification, the Dewey decimal classification, or a locally-developed scheme. Accession numbers may be used. The ALA guidelines recommend that the class number "should be determined from what the software is about rather than the fact that it is software" (p. 6).

Classification numbers in this manual are from the latest LC class schedules and their supplements.

MARC CODING AND TAGGING BIBLIOGRAPHIC RECORDS FOR OCLC INPUT

The MARC coding and tagging of examples in this manual is done according to *Computer Files Format*, (OCLC, 1989) with update through August 1992.

Only those MARC codes and tags specific to computer files are covered here. The OCLC version of the MARC format for computer files is explained and illustrated. Monographic computer files are discussed first, then serial computer files.

Fixed fields

File

"File" is a one-character code that indicates the type of computer file being described. Codes available include:

a   Numeric file
      A computer file containing mostly numbers or representations by numbers. May be
      original data, summary data, or statistically manipulated data

b   Computer programs
      All types of computer programs

c   Representational file
      Pictorial or graphic information

d   Text file
      A computer file containing written text or bibliographic information in coded form. The
      text of a computer program (the programming language itself) is not considered to be text
      for the purpose of this fixed field code

m   Combination
      Any combination of the above

u   Unknown

z   Other

Lang

This field is encoded for the language of the work. It is only applied, however, to the language of text files. The language apparent to the user (title screens, menu, instructions, etc.) is ignored, as is the programming language.

For most computer files, therefore, the value used for this code will be "N/A" for not applicable. Field 041 is used for the language of manuals, guides, etc.

This practice will change soon, and the fixed field will contain the code for the language of the title and credits screens (or the chief source of information), just as we code all other media except music. This change was discussed at the MARBI meetings during the ALA Annual Conference held in June 1992. The implementation of the change will be announced later.

Examples in this manual will be coded with the language code in the fixed field rather than in an 041.

Type

The only code permitted for "Type," type of record, is "m" for machine-readable data file, the term formerly used for computer files.

Audience

Intellectual level for computer files is now defined for byte 2 of field 008. The values used are the same as used in the Visual Materials Format (OCLC's Audiovisual Media Format). Those values are:

a   preschool
b   primary
      kindergarten-grade 3
c   elementary and junior high
      grades 4-8
d   secondary
      grades 9-12
e   adult
f   specialized
g   general (fiction)
blank for not applicable or unknown

Variable Fields

041 Languages

Language or languages represented in a computer file, at present, are expressed using field 041. The first indicator shows whether the computer file is or includes a translation, with "0" for items that are not translations and "1" for items that are translations or that include translations. The second indicator is blank.

There are five subfields;

a   for language of the text
b   language of summaries or abstracts
f   language of table of contents
g   language of accompanying material
h   for language of original and/or intermediate translations of text

For most computer files, fixed field "Lang" is coded "N/A." Field 041 has a first indicator of 0. Subfield ‡g in field 041 contains the code for English.

Soon language will be coded in the fixed field as for other material — see discussion under "Lang."

245 GMD

The GMD is input into subfield ‡h *without* square brackets in accordance with OCLC practice. If a specific system does not supply square brackets around the GMD in subfield ‡h, they will need to be input explicitly by the cataloger.

256 File Characteristics

Field 256 has been established for the information appearing in area 3, "File characteristics," of the bibliographic record. There are no indicators and no subfield codes other than subfield ‡a.

530 Additional Physical Forms Available

Field 530 contains information about additional physical format(s) in which the materials are available for use, at the repository and/or in published form. If describing a published form, field 530 also contains information about the availability source and the order number of the published form.

538 Technical Details Note

All technical information about the computer file goes in field 538. The field is repeatable; one 538 may be used for the system requirements note, another for disk characteristics.

There are no indicators for this field.

There is no print constant associated with the field. The words "System requirements:" or "Disk characteristics:" must be input as needed. The text is input exactly as it is to appear. Subfield ǂa is the only subfield code for this field.

630, 730 Uniform Titles

The Library of Congress announced in *Cataloging Service Bulletin* 38 (fall 1987) that headings for computer programs and software should be treated as uniform titles. Subject headings for names of computer programs or software would be assigned the tag 630, with second indicator zero. Names of computer programming languages and computer systems continue to be entered in field 650.

An added entry made for a specific computer program would be tagged as field 730 rather than field 740. Added entries for variant titles, however, would be tagged as field 740.

Authority records in the LC Authority File will be established as uniform titles in field 130, although many still appear in field 150. These older headings will be changed as needed.

753 Technical Details Access

Field 753 provides access to technical details about the computer file. Subfield ǂa is for make and model of computer. Subfield ǂb is for programming language, and subfield ǂc for operating system.

The field is repeatable.

SERIALS

Serial computer files may be cataloged on OCLC as computer files, using the computer file version of the OCLC workform, or as serials, using the serial version of the workform. In either case certain data elements cannot be input. The OCLC computer file format accomodates the following data elements for serials:

Bib lvl	Bibliographic level
Dates	
Frequn	Frequency
Pub st	Publication status
Regulr	Regularity
315	Frequency
362	Area 3 information

Bib lvl

In the fixed field "Bib lvl" for bibliographic level, two codes are available for use with serials:

    s   serial
    b   component part, serial

Dates

In the "Dates" fixed field the comma is replaced by a hyphen when the workform is reformatted, if Bib lvl contains "s" or "b".

Frequn

In the "Frequn" fixed field a one-character code identifies the frequency of publication. There are 19 codes available for use in this field.

Pub st

Publication status, "Pub st" in the fixed field, contains a one-character code indicating whether the serial is currently being published. This code displays only after Bib lvl has been filled in and the workform reformatted. Values available include:

    c   currently published
    d   dead
    u   unknown

Regulr

Regularity, "Regulr", is represented by a one-character code in the fixed fields. Values available include:

    r   material published at regular intervals
    n   normalized irregular (material published irregularly in a predictable pattern)
    x   completely irregular
    u   unknown

The value used for this code should agree with the code used for frequency of the serial.

315 Frequency

Field 315 is used for frequency of the serial computer file.

362 Numeric and/or Alphabetic, Chronological, or Other Designation

Field 362 is used for information found in area 3 of serials cataloging. An indicator tells whether the field is in formatted style or in unformatted style. Formatted style will appear as area 3 information on a printed card; unformatted style will appear as a note.

LIBRARY OF CONGRESS
CATALOGING OF COMPUTER FILES

The following example taken from OCLC shows LC cataloging of a computer file.

```
Type: m        Bib lvl: m Source: d    Lang: N/A
File: b        Enc lvl: I Govt pub:    Ctry: mnu
Audience: f Mod rec:    Frequen: n  Regulr:
Desc: a        Dat tp: s Dates: 1987,
  1 010        87-5924
  2 040        DLC ǂc CSS ǂd m/c ǂd OCL
  3 020        0874903947 : ǂc $49.00 ($55.00 for 3 1/2 in. disk)
  4 041 0      ǂg eng
  5 050 0      PE1175 ǂb .W73 1987
  6 082        372.4/144
  7 090        ǂb
  8 049        MNMA
  9 245 00     Words at work. ǂp Compound it! ǂh computer file
 10 250        Version 1.0
 11 260        St. Paul, Minn. : ǂb Minnesota Educational Computing Corp., ǂc
c1987.
 12 300        1 computer disk : ǂb sd., col. ; ǂc 5 1/4 in. + ǂe 1 manual.
 13 440  0     MECC reading collection
 14 490 1      Word-building series
 15 538        System requirements: Apple II; 64K; DOS 3.3; BASIC; 1 disk drive;
monochrome or color monitor; printer optional.
 16 500        Title from title screen.
 17 500        Edition statement from disk label.
 18 521        Grades 3-6.
 19 500        Issued also on 3 1/2 in. computer disk.
 20 520        A clown and a cowpoke lead the way as children develop their
skills at recognizing, understanding, and using compound words. Features over
one hundred and seventy compounds in a package of educational games and drills.
 21 505 0      Clown around -- Cowbell -- The compound game.
 22 500        "A183"--Disk label.
 23 650  0     English language ǂx Compound words ǂx Juvenile software.
 24 650  0     English language ǂx Word formation ǂx Juvenile software.
 25 650  0     Reading (Elementary) ǂx Juvenile software.
 26 650  1     English language ǂx Compound words ǂx Software.
 27 650  1     Readers ǂx Software.
 28 650  8     Reading.
 29 650  8     Vocabulary.
 30 710 20     Minnesota Educational Computing Corporation. ǂw cn
 31 740 01     Compound it!
 32 830  0     Word-building series.
```

Examples

The examples in this manual show cataloging with many kinds of title problems, great variety in edition statements, and hundreds of notes. There are examples with different editions of a title, examples needing a uniform title, and examples with one or more title added entries. There is an example of a book with a disk, one that is a disk with a book, and one that could be either (or could be a kit; it depends how one looks at it). There are regular computer disk, compact disks, and interactive disks. There are files with no disks, available only by remote access.

There are monographs, serials, and "in" analytics. Some examples are cataloged more than one way: as a set or as an item in the set; as a serial or as a monograph.

Some examples are old and date from the first software I handled. I keep using them because the title screens are clear and show information that needs to be explained. I also keep using them because I no longer have the capability to "capture" the Apple or Mac screens.

I have tried to include examples showing every kind of problem one might encounter in cataloging computer files, although I realize new problems develop as fast as, or faster than, we solve the ones in hand.

The new technology is exciting. Interactive material allows the user to control the process of retrieving information, much like skimming through a pile of books, pulling out bits here and there as interested, only in a computer environment with all types of media at hand. And all may be packaged on a single physical item.

The ability to catalog online resources opens up the possibilities of access to many more items, while it presents problems for catalogers. However, the current rules allow us to catalog items available by remote access, and the MARC format is flexible, so we can at least try. I do not include cataloging of Internet files in this manual because decisions still are to be made on how to handle addresses and local information. The files may be described adequately using current rules, but access information (kind and amount) has yet to be worked out.

Example 1

Title screen

Example 1

```
Lutus, Paul.
     MusiComp [computer file] / by Paul Lutus. -- Computer program.
-- Cupertino, Calif. : Apple Computer, c1980.
     1 computer disk : sd., col. ; 5 1/4 in. + 1 manual (22 p. ; 22
cm.). -- (Special delivery software)

     System requirements: Apple II.
     Title from title screen.
     Summary: Uses the Apple's sound generating capability to play
music and displays the musical notes on the screen. Also allows
user to program in compositions.
```

```
     1. Composition (Music).  I. Apple Computer, Inc.  II. Title.
III. Title: Music comp.  IV. Series.  V. Apple II.


     MT40
```

This program has an author clearly named on the title screen. The authorship statement is transcribed as a statement of responsibility.

The title is made up of two words put together with an embedded capital letter. An added entry should be made for the two-word title as well as for the one-word title, if some users might look for the title as two words.

In area 3, the word "computer" is optional if a GMD is used. LC would not use area 3 for this example.

Rules for notes are, in order, 9.7B1b, 9.7B3, 9.7B17.

```
Type: m      Bib lvl: m Source: d   Lang: eng
File: b      Enc lvl: I Govt pub:   Ctry: cau
Audience: f Mod rec:    Frequen: n  Regulr:
Desc: a      Dat tp: s  Dates: 1980,
 1 010
 2 040       XXX ǂc XXX
 3 090       MT40
 4 049       XXXX
 5 100 1     Lutus, Paul.
 6 245 10    MusiComp ǂh computer file / ǂc by Paul Lutus.
 7 256       Computer program.
 8 260       Cupertino, Calif. : ǂb Apple Computer, ǂc c1980.
 9 300       1 computer disk : ǂb sd., col. ; ǂc 5 1/4 in. + ǂe 1 manual (22 p. ;
22 cm.)
10 440 0     Special delivery software
11 538       System requirements: Apple II.
12 500       Title from title screen.
13 520       Uses the Apple's sound generating capability to play music and
displays the musical notes on the screen. Also allows user to program in
compositions.
14 650  0    Composition (Music)
15 710 20    Apple Computer, Inc.
16 740 01    Music comp.
17 753       Apple II.
```

Example 2

Title screens

```
1. Trap and Guess
2. Bumblebug
3. Hidden Treasure
4. Bumble Art
5. Roadblock


6. Sound on/off

7. End
```

From the manual

WELCOME TO BUMBLE PLOT

Meet Bumble, a friendly creature from the planet Furrin, who has some challenging games for you. Each game helps you learn to identify points on lines and grids. You will need this skill to find places on maps and to read or make charts and graphs. Bumble will also help you understand the meaning of negative and positive numbers and to see what is meant by a number being greater or less than another.

Play the games and you will become a powerful number-pair plotter! You can also learn about computer graphics as you draw pictures with your computer.

If this is the first time you have used Bumble Plot, start at the beginning and take your time. Play each game in order so you can learn everything step by step.

P.S. Some people may think that Bumble Plot is just for fun. To see what you are learning, turn to THE LEARNING LIST on page 18.

Example 2

```
Grimm, Leslie.
     Bumble plot [computer file] / by Leslie Grimm ; artist,
Corinne. -- V[ersion] 1.1. -- Programs. -- Portolo Valley, Calif.
: The Learning Company, c1982.
     1 computer disk : sd., col. ; 5 1/4 in. + 1 manual. --
(Computer learning games)

     System requirements: Apple II.
     Title from title screen.
     Summary: Five educational games to help user (age 8-13)
identify points on lines and grids.
     Contents: 1. Trap and guess -- 2. Bumblebug -- 3. Hidden
treasure -- 4. Bumble art -- 5. Roadblock.
```

```
     1. Computer graphics.  2. Games in mathematics education.  I.
Learning Company.  II. Apple II.  III. Title.  IV. Title: Trap and
guess.  V. Title: Bumblebug.  VI. Title: Hidden treasure. VII.
Title: Bumble art. VIII. Title: Roadblock. IX. Series.

     QA115
```

Area 3 is used here without the optional repetition of the word "computer".

Descriptions of the separate games are not needed for this cataloging as the single summary sufficiently describes the subject matter of the package.

Rules for notes are, in order, 9.7B1b, 9.7B3, 9.7B17, 9.7B18.

```
Type: m      Bib lvl: m Source: d    Lang: eng
File: m      Enc lvl: I Govt pub:    Ctry: cau
Audience: c Mod rec:    Frequen: n   Regulr:
Desc: a      Dat tp: s  Dates: 1982,
 1 010
 2 040      XXX ǂc XXX
 3 090      QA115
 4 049      XXXX
 5 100 1    Grimm, Leslie.
 6 245 10   Bumble plot ǂh computer file / ǂc by Leslie Grimm ; artist, Corinne.
 7 250      V[ersion] 1.1.
 8 256      Programs.
 9 260      Portolo Valley, Calif. : ǂb The Learning Company, ǂc c1982.
10 300      1 computer disk : ǂb sd., col. ; ǂc 5 1/4 in. + ǂe 1 manual.
11 440   0  Computer learning games
12 538      System requirements: Apple II.
13 500      Title from title screen.
14 520      Five educational games to help user (age 8-13) identify points on
lines and grids.
15 505 0    1. Trap and guess -- 2. Bumblebug -- 3. Hidden treasure -- 4. Bumble
art -- 5. Roadblock.
16 650   0  Computer graphics.
17 650   0  Games in mathematics education.
18 710 20   Learning Company.
19 753      Apple II.
20 740 02   Trap and guess.
```
(Continued on next page)

```
21 740 02  Bumblebug.
22 740 02  Hidden treasure.
23 740 02  Bumble art.
24 740 02  Roadblock.
```

Example 3

Title screen transcriptions

```
┌─────────────────────────────────────────┐
│                 Kid Pix                   │
│         © 1991 Craig Hickman and          │
│         Broderbund Software, Inc.         │
│            All Rights Reserved.           │
│               Version 1.1                 │
└─────────────────────────────────────────┘
```

```
┌─────────────────────────────────────────────────────────┐
│              Program by Craig Hickman                      │
│           Product Manager Leslie Hickman                   │
│       Graphics Michelle Bushneff, Craig Hickman            │
│  Sound Jonelle Adkisson, Craig Hickman, Tom Rettig         │
│              Manual Susan Meyers                           │
└─────────────────────────────────────────────────────────┘
```

```
┌─────────────────────────────────────────┐
│         Color printing technology         │
│       Copyright © 1990 Equilibrium        │
│        Programmed by Dave Theurer         │
└─────────────────────────────────────────┘
```

```
┌─────────────────────────────────────────┐
│              With Thanks To:              │
│               [30 people]                 │
└─────────────────────────────────────────┘
```

```
┌─────────────────────────────────────────┐
│               Kid Pix Fans:               │
│         [children of the 30 people]       │
└─────────────────────────────────────────┘
```

Example 3

```
Kid pix [computer file]. -- Version 1.1. -- San Rafael, Calif. :
    Broderbund, c1991.
        2 computer disks : sd., col. ; 3 1/2 in. + 1 user's guide +
    1 sheet of stickers.

        "The paint program just for kids"--Container.
        System requirements: Macintosh; hard disk or two 800K disk
    drives; color printer optional.
        Spoken alphabet available in Spanish or English.
        Title from title screen.
        Program by Craig Hickman; graphics, Michelle Bushneff, Craig
    Hickman; sound, Jonell Adkisson, Craig Hickman, Tom Rettig;
    manual, Susan Meyers.
        "Color printing technology programmed by Dave Theurer, c1990
    Equilibrium."
        Second disk is "bonus sounds."
        ISBN 1-55790-581-9.


        1. Computer art.  I. Hickman, Craig.  II. Theurer, Dave.
    III. Broderbund Software, Inc.  IV. Equilibrium (Firm)  V.
    Macintosh.

    N7433.8
```

As computer technology develops and becomes more complex, responsiblity for the contents of a given package becomes more diffuse. The two 9.7B6 notes give the major statements of responsibility found on the credit screens and in the manual.

Audience is coded for the highest level applicable. I chose to use "c" for elementary and junior high.

Rules for notes are, in order, 9.7B1a, 9.7B1b, 9.7B2, 9.7B3, 9.7B6, 9.7B6, 9.7B10.

```
Type: m      Bib lvl: m Source: d    Lang: eng
File: m      Enc lvl: I Govt pub:    Ctry: cau
Audience: c Mod rec:    Frequen: n  Regulr:
Desc: a      Dat tp: s  Dates: 1991,
 1 010
 2 020      1557905819
 3 040      XXX ‡c XXX
 4 090      N7433.8
 5 049      XXXX
 6 245 10   Kid pix ‡h computer file
 7 250      Version 1.1.
 8 260      San Rafael, Calif. : ‡b Broderbund, ‡c c1991.
 9 300      2 computer disks : ‡b sd., col. : ‡c 3 1/2 in. + ‡e 1 user's guide +
1 sheet of stickers.
10 500      "The paint program just for kids"--Container.
11 538      System requirements: Macintosh; hard disk or two 800K disk drives;
color printer optional.
12 500      Spoken alphabet available in Spanish or English.
13 500      Title from title screen.
```
(Continued on next page)

14 500   Program by Craig Hickman; graphics, Michelle Bushneff, Craig Hickman;
sound, Jonell Adkisson, Craig Hickman, Tom Rettig; manual, Susan Meyers.
15 500   "Color printing technology programmed by Dave Theurer, c1990
Equilibrium."
16 500   Second disk is "bonus sounds."
17 650 0 Computer art.
18 710 20 Broderbund Software, Inc.
19 710 20 Equilibrium (Firm)
20 753   Macintosh.

Example 4

Title screen

MacDraw Version*91 1/24/85

by Mark Cutter

© 1984 Apple Computer Inc.

	Active Document	All
Number of objects:	0	0
Percent of Memory Used:	0	0

OK

Example 4

```
Cutter, Mark.
    MacDraw [computer file] / by Mark Cutter. -- Version*91. --
Cupertino, Calif. : Apple Computer, 1985.
    1 computer disk ; 3 1/2 in. + 1 manual (120 p. : ill. ; 23 cm.)

    System requirements: Macintosh; 128K; printer.
    Title from title screen.
    Summary: Allows user to create precise complex drawings that
can be changed and modified.


    1. Computer graphics.  I. Apple Computer, Inc.  II. Macintosh.
III. Title.

    T385
```

The edition statement includes an asterisk, just as it appeared in the chief source of information. Notes are created according to rules 9.7B1b, 9.7B3, and 9.7B17.

```
Type: m       Bib lvl: m Source: d    Lang: eng
File: b       Enc lvl: I Govt pub:    Ctry: cau
Audience: f Mod rec:     Frequen: n Regulr:
Desc: a.      Dat tp: s Dates: 1985,
  1 010
  2 040      XXX ǂc XXX
  3 090      T385
  4 049      XXXX
  5 100 1    Cutter, Mark.
  6 245 10   MacDraw ǂh computer file / ǂc by Mark Cutter.
  7 250      Version*91.
  8 260      Cupertino, Calif. : ǂb Apple Computer, ǂc 1985.
  9 300      1 computer disk ; ǂc 3 1/2 in. + ǂe 1 manual (120 p. : ill. ; 23cm.)
 10 538      System requirements: Macintosh; 128K; printer.
 11 500      Title from title screen.
 12 520      Allows user to create precise complex drawings that can be changed
and modified.
 13 650  0   Computer graphics.
 14 710 20   Apple Computer, Inc.
 15 753      Macintosh.
```

Example 5

Title screens

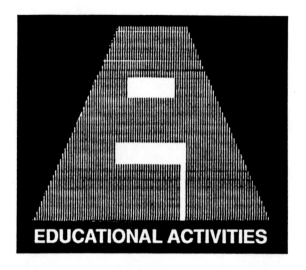

EDUCATIONAL ACTIVITIES

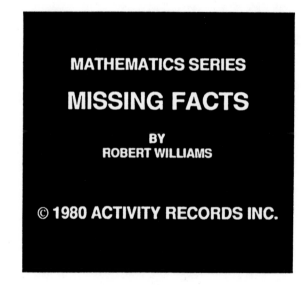

MATHEMATICS SERIES

MISSING FACTS

BY
ROBERT WILLIAMS

© 1980 ACTIVITY RECORDS INC.

Example 5

```
Williams, Robert.
    Missing facts [computer file] / by Robert Williams. --
Freeport, N.Y. : Educational Activities, c1980.
    1 computer disk : col. ; 5 1/4 in. -- (Mathematics series)

    System requirements: Apple II.
    Title from title screen.
    Also called: Missing math facts.
    Copyright by Activity Records Inc.
    Summary: Includes examples for addition, subtraction,
multiplication, and division with four levels of difficulty for
each process.


    1. Arithmetic.  I. Educational Activities (Firm)  II. Activity
Records Inc.  III. Apple II.  IV. Title.  V. Title: Missing math
facts.

QA115
```

The copyright note is included because this firm is noted prominently on the title screen, and an added entry should be made for it. A person or body must be named somewhere in the bibliographic record to justify an added entry, thus the note.

Rules for notes are 9.7B1b, 9.7B3, 9.7B4, 9.7B6, 9.7B17.

```
Type: m      Bib lvl: m Source: d   Lang: eng
File: m      Enc lvl: I Govt pub:   Ctry: nyu
Audience: c Mod rec:    Frequen: n  Regulr:
Desc: a      Dat tp: s  Dates: 1980,
 1 010
 2 040     XXX ǂc XXX
 3 090     QA115
 4 049     XXXX
 5 100  1  Williams, Robert.
 6 245 10  Missing facts ǂh computer file / ǂc by Robert Williams.
 7 260     Freeport, N.Y. : ǂb Educational Activities, ǂc c1980.
 8 300     1 computer disk : ǂb col. ; ǂc 5 1/4 in.
 9 440  0  Mathematics series
10 538     System requirements: Apple II.
11 500     Title from title screen.
12 500     Also called: Missing math facts.
13 500     Copyright by Activity Records Inc.
14 520     Includes examples for addition, subtraction, multiplication, and
division with four levels of difficulty for each process.
15 650  0  Arithmetic.
16 710 20  Educational Activities (Firm)
17 710 20  Activity Records Inc.
18 753     Apple II.
19 740 01  Missing math facts.
```

34

Example 6

Manual title page

IBM-PC
and Major Compatibles

AUDITING-THEORY
BUSINESS LAW
PRACTICE

EXAMINATION REVIEW

MICROCOMPUTER
DIAGNOSTICS
1985 EDITION

Irvin N. Gleim
Patrick R. Delaney

ISBN 0-471-82338-4

From the manual

WHAT IS CPAMD?

CPAMD is a software program that provides you with a flexible environment in which you can interact with sets of multiple-choice questions drawn from the last four years. The design of the program is to give control over the questions and the process of interacting with them.

You should view the operation of the program as having three levels. At the top level, you select a question set be reviewing the description of the contents of each. At the next level, having selected a question set, you can then rearrange the questions in that set and, on demand, select questions that you want to view. Finally, at the lowest level, having selected a question you can select an answer to it and optionally view the rationale for that answer.

The program allows you to interact with the questions in either a STUDY REVIEW mode or an EXAM mode.

WHAT DOES CPAMD CONTAIN?

Your CPAMD package contains the following:
- Disk I — Auditing and Accounting Theory
- Disk II — Business Law
- Disk III — Accounting Practice
- User Manual
- Registration Card and Licensing Agreement
- Key Command Card

Example 6

Title screen

```
┌─────────────────────────────────────┐
│          Gleim & Delaney            │
│                                      │
│            C P A M D                 │
│                                      │
│           1985 Edition               │
│                                      │
│       Published by John Wiley        │
│        All Rights Reserved           │
│         Copyright 1985               │
└─────────────────────────────────────┘
```

```
Gleim, Irvin N.
    CPAMD [computer file] / Gleim & Delaney. -- 1985 ed. -- New
York : J. Wiley, c1985.
    3 computer disks ; 5 1/4 in. + 1 manual (30 p. ; 23 cm.)

    System requirements: IBM PC; MS-DOS 2.0.
    Title from title screen.
    Manual: CPA examination review : microcomputer diagnostics /
Irvin N. Gleim, Patrick R. Delaney.
    Summary: Includes sets of questions on auditing, accounting
theory, business law, and accounting practice, the four main
topics of the CPA examination.


    1. Accountants--Examinations, questions, etc.  I. Gleim, Irvin
N.  CPA examination review. 1985.  II. IBM PC.  III. Title.

HF5627
```

Note the wording and punctuation of the note referring to the accompanying manual that was by the same publisher as the disk (1.7B11, 1.7A3).

Rules for notes are 9.7B1b, 9.7B3, 9.7B11, 9.7B17.

```
Type: m       Bib lvl: m Source: d   Lang: eng
File: m       Enc lvl: I Govt pub:   Ctry: nyu
Audience: f Mod rec:     Frequen: n  Regulr:
Desc: a       Dat tp: s Dates: 1985,
 1 010
 2 040     XXX ǂc XXX
 3 090     HF5627
 4 049     XXXX
 5 100 1   Gleim, Irvin N.
 6 245 10  CPAMD ǂh computer file / ǂc Gleim & Delaney.
 7 250     1985 ed.
 8 260     New York : ǂb J. Wiley, ǂc c1985.
```
(Continued on next page)

```
 9 300     3 computer disks ; ǂc 5 1/4 in. + ǂe 1 manual (30 p. ; 23 cm.)
10 538     System requirements: IBM PC; MS-DOS 2.0.
11 500     Title from title screen.
12 500     Manual: CPA examination review : microcomputer diagnostics / Irvin N.
Gleim, Patrick R. Delaney.
13 520     Includes sets of questions on auditing, accounting theory, business
law, and accounting practice, the four main topics of the CPA examination.
14 650   0 Accountants ǂx Examinations, questions, etc.
15 700  12 Gleim, Irvin N. ǂt CPA examination review. ǂf 1985.
16 753     IBM PC.
```

Example 7

Title screens

```
                              Catlab

                              A Genetics Simulation


              J. F. Kinnear
              Melbourne State College, Australia

              A CONDUIT Reviewed and Tested Package
              Copyright 1982 by J. F. Kinnear
```

```
         © 1982  Judith Kinnear, Melbourne State College

         CATLAB is published by CONDUIT, P.O. Box 388, Iowa City, IA 52244.

         Apple Computer, Inc. makes no warranties, either express or implied,
    regarding the computer software associated with CATLAB package, its mer-
    chantability or its fitness for any particular purpose.  "Apple" or "Apple
    II" iws th eregistered trademark of Apple Computer, Inc.

         Partial support for preparation of this material for districtution was
    provided by the Fund for the Imporvement of Postsecondary Education, Grant
    G007905216.  Any opinions, findings, conclusions, or recommendations
    expressed or implied here do not necessarily reflect the views of the
    Foundation.
```

Disk label

Conduit   BIO319A: CATLAB
COMPUTING IDEAS FOR EDUCATION   APPLESOFT 48k, DOS 3.3

If for any reason you cannot read this diskette, contact CONDUIT immediately for authorization to exchange (319-353-5789).
Replacement will be made free of charge, if requested within 30 days of date shipped.
© CONDUIT P.O. Box 388, Iowa City, IA 52244   **Duplicate for backup only**

Example 7

```
Kinnear, J. F. (Judith F.)
    Catlab [computer file] : a genetics simulation / J.F. Kinnear.
-- Iowa City, IA : Conduit, c1982.
    1 computer disk : sd., col. ; 5 1/4 in. + 8 col. slides + 1
student guide (29 p. : ill. ; 21 cm.) + 1 instructor manual (39 p.
: ill. ; 21 cm.)

    System requirements: Apple II; slide projector.
    Title from title screen.
    Slides show cat-coat colors and patterns.
    Summary: Teaches principles of genetics through a simulation in
which cats of different coat color and pattern are mated.


    1. Genetics, Experimental.  I. Conduit (Firm)  II. Apple II.
III. Title.

QL738.5
```

This item has slides to be used with it. It is not a kit because the computer material is the dominant item; the slides are accompanying material.

Rules for notes are 9.7B1b, 9.7B3, 9.7B11, 9.7B17.

```
Type: m       Bib lvl: m Source: d    Lang: eng
File: m       Enc lvl: I Govt pub:    Ctry: iau
Audience: f Mod rec:    Frequen: n  Regulr:
Desc: a       Dat tp: s  Dates: 1982,
 1 010
 2 040     XXX ‡c XXX
 3 090     QL738.5
 4 049     XXXX
 5 100 1   Kinnear, J. F. ‡q (Judith F.)
 6 245 10  Catlab ‡h computer file : ‡b a genetics simulation / ‡c J.F. Kinnear.
 7 260     Iowa City, IA : ‡b Conduit, ‡c c1982.
 8 300     1 computer disk : ‡b sd., col. ; ‡c 5 1/4 in. + ‡e 8 col. slides + 1
student guide (29 p. : ill. ; 21 cm.) + 1 instructor manual (39 p. : ill. ;
21cm.)
 9 538     System requirements: Apple II; slide projector.
10 500     Title from title screen.
11 500     Slides show cat-coat colors and patterns.
12 520     Teaches principles of genetics through a simulation in which cats of
different coat color and pattern are mated.
13 650  0 Genetics, Experimental.
14 710 20 Conduit (Firm)
15 753    Apple II.
```

Example 8

Title screen

Manual title page

Example 8

```
Corl, Terry.
    Quick-search librarian [computer file] / by Terry Corl & Paul
K. Warme. -- Version 1.1. -- State College, Pa. : Interactive
Microware, c1982.
    1 computer disk ; 5 1/4 in. + 1 instruction manual.

    System requirements: Apple II; printer.
    Title from title screen.
    Summary: Allows user to create a personal database containing
references to journals. References can be entered, edited,
searched, sorted, and printed.


    1. Information storage and retrieval systems.  2. Bibliographic
citations--Computer programs  I. Warme, Paul K.  II. Interactive
Microware, Inc.  III. Apple II.  IV. Title.  V. Title: Quick
search librarian.

Z1001
```

Note the transcription of the statement of responsibility exactly as it appears on the title screen, with the "&".

A title added entry with "Quick search" as two words would be needed in an online catalog that treats a hyphenated word as one word rather than as two words.

Rules for notes are 9.7B1b, 9.7B3, 9.7B17.

```
Type: m       Bib lvl: m Source: d    Lang: eng
File: b       Enc lvl: I Govt pub:    Ctry: pau
Audience: f Mod rec:    Frequen: n  Regulr:
Desc: a       Dat tp: s  Dates: 1982,
 1 010
 2 040     XXX ǂc XXX
 3 090     Z1001
 4 049     XXXX
 5 100 1   Corl, Terry.
 6 245 10  Quick-search librarian ǂh computer file / by Terry Corl & Paul K.
Warme.
 7 250     Version 1.1.
 8 260     State College, Pa. : ǂb Interactive Microware, ǂc c1982.
 9 300     1 computer disk ; ǂc 5 1/4 in. + ǂe 1 instruction manual.
10 538     System requirements: Apple II; printer.
11 500     Title from title screen.
12 520     Allows user to create a personal database containing references to
journals. References can be entered, edited, searched, sorted, and printed.
13 650 0   Information storage and retrieval systems.
14 650  0  Bibliographic citations ǂx Computer programs.
15 700 10  Warme, Paul K.
16 710 20  Interactive Microware, Inc.
17 753     Apple II.
18 740 01  Quick search librarian.
```

Example 9

Title screen

The ❋ ❋ ❋

BANK STREET

❋ Writer™ ❋

Developed by
Intentional Educations, Inc.
Franklin E. Smith and
(C) 1982 The Bank Street College
of Education
Programmer: Gene Kusmiak

BRODERBUND SOFTWARE, INC.

Example 9

```
The Bank Street writer [computer file] / developed by Intentional
    Educations, Inc., Franklin E. Smith, and the Bank Street
    College of Education ; programmer, Gene Kusmiak. -- San Rafael,
    Calif. : Broderbund Software, c1982.
        1 computer disk ; 5 1/4 in. + 1 manual.

        Word processing system.
        System requirements: Apple II; printer.
        Title from title screen.


        1. Word processing.  I. Smith, Franklin E.  II. Intentional
    Educations, Inc.  III. Bank Street College of Education.  IV.
    Broderbund Software (Firm)  V. Apple II.

    Z52.5.B3
```

The nature and scope note is the only note to precede the system requirements note.

Rules for notes are 9.7B1a, 9.7B1b, 9.7B3. No summary is needed, because the nature and scope note is sufficient explanation.

```
Type: m      Bib lvl: m Source: d   Lang: eng
File: b      Enc lvl: I Govt pub:   Ctry: cau
Audience: f Mod rec:    Frequen: n  Regulr:
Desc: a      Dat tp: s Dates: 1982,
 1 010
 2 040     XXX ǂc XXX
 3 090     Z52.5.B3
 4 049     XXXX
 5 245 04  The Bank Street writer ǂh computer file / ǂc developed by Intentional
Educations, Inc., Franklin E. Smith, and the Bank Street College of Education ;
programmer, Gene Kusmiak.
 6 260     San Rafael, Calif. : ǂb Broderbund Software, ǂc c1982.
 7 300     1 computer disk ; ǂc 5 1/4 in. + ǂe 1 manual.
 8 500     Word processing system.
 9 538     System requirements: Apple II; printer.
10 500     Title from title screen.
11 650   0 Word processing.
12 700 10  Smith, Franklin E.
13 710 20  Intentional Educations, Inc.
14 710 20  Bank Street College of Education.
15 710 20  Broderbund Software (Firm)
16 753     Apple II.
```

42

Example 10

Title screen

```
╔══════════════════════════════════════════════════════╗
║ ▤□▦▦▦▦▦▦▦ Omnis 3 Database Manager ▦▦▦▦▦▦▦ ║
╠══════════════════════════════════════════════════════╣
║                                                        ║
║        Version number: 3.10.MAC                        ║
║                                                        ║
║        Serial number:  Shown on disk label             ║
║                                                        ║
║        Supplied to:                                    ║
║          Olson                                         ║
║                                                        ║
║        Supplied by:                                    ║
║          BLYTH SOFTWARE INC                            ║
║          2655 CAMPUS DRIVE #150                         ║
║          SAN MATEO, CA 94403                           ║
║                                                        ║
║        (C) BLYTH SOFTWARE LIMITED  1985                ║
║                                                        ║
╚══════════════════════════════════════════════════════╝
```

Example 10

```
Omnis 3 database manager [computer file]. -- Version number
    3.10.MAC. -- San Mateo, CA : Blyth Software, c1985.
        4 computer disks ; 3 1/2 in. + 1 manual + 1 pocket reference
    guide.

        System requirements: Macintosh; 512K; hard disk drive;
    printer.
        Title from title screen.
        Title of manual: Omnis 3, the database manager.
        One disk is backup.


        1. Data base management.  I. Blyth Software Limited.  II.
    Omnis 3, the database manager. 1985. III. Macintosh.  IV.
    Title: Omnis three database manager.

    QA76.9.D3
```

The form of name chosen for the first added entry was taken from the copyright statement. Blyth Software is not in LC's authority file as of Feb. 9, 1992.
Rules for notes are 9.7B1b, 9.7B3, 9.7B4, 9.7B10.

```
Type: m      Bib lvl: m Source: d   Lang: eng
File: b      Enc lvl: I Govt pub:   Ctry: cau
Audience: f Mod rec:   Frequen: n  Regulr:
Desc: a      Dat tp: s  Dates: 1985,
 1 010
 2 040      XXX ǂc XXX
 3 090      QA76.9.D3
 4 049      XXXX
 5 245 00   Omnis 3 database manager ǂh computer file
 6 250      Version number 3.10.MAC.
 7 260      San Mateo, CA : ǂb Blyth Software, ǂc c1985.
 8 300      4 computer disks ; ǂc 3 1/2 in. + ǂe 1 manual + 1 pocket
referenceguide.
 9 538      System requirements: Macintosh; 512K; hard disk drive; printer.
10 500      Title from title screen.
11 500      Title of manual: Omnis 3, the database manager.
12 500      One disk is backup.
13 650  0   Data base management.
14 710 20   Blyth Software Limited.
15 730 02   Omnis 3, the database manager. ǂf 1985.
16 753      Macintosh.
17 740 01   Omnis three database manager.
```

44

Example 11

Title screen

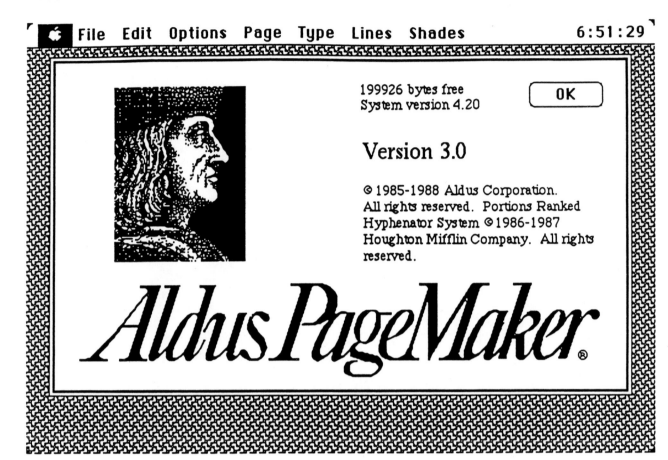

Example 11

```
Aldus pagemaker [computer file] / written by Jeremy Jaech ... [et
    al.]. -- Version 3.0. -- Seattle, Wash. : Aldus, 1988.
        5 computer disks : col. ; 3 1/2 in. + 3 manuals.

        System requirements: Apple Macintosh II or Apple Macintosh
    SE or Apple Macintosh Plus and a hard disk drive; or Apple
    Macintosh 512K Enhanced with 1 megabyte of memory and a hard
    disk drive; Apple System 4.1 and Finder 5.5 or later;
    ImageWriter, color ImageWriter, or LaserWriter printer, or
    other PostScript compatible device.
        Title from title screen.
        Summary: Formats pages of newsletters, newspapers, and
    documents for printing.


        1. Desktop publishing.  I. Jaech, Jeremy.  II. Aldus
    Corporation.  III. Macintosh.  IV. Title: Pagemaker.  V. Title:
    Page maker.

        Z286.D47
```

The systems requirements note is unusually long, but that's the information the patron needs.
Rules for notes are 9.7B1b, 9.7B3, 9.7B17.

```
Type: m      Bib lvl: m Source: d    Lang: eng
File: b      Enc lvl: I Govt pub:    Ctry: wau
Audience: f Mod rec:    Frequen: n  Regulr:
Desc: a      Dat tp: s  Dates: 1988,
 1 010
 2 040       XXX ‡c XXX
 3 090       Z286.D47
 4 049       XXXX
 5 245 00 Aldus pagemaker ‡h computer file / ‡c written by Jeremy Jaech ... [et
al.].
 6 250       Version 3.0.
 7 260       Seattle, Wash. : ‡b Aldus, ‡c 1988.
 8 300       5 computer disks : ‡b ; ‡c 3 1/2 in. + ‡e 3 manuals.
 9 538       System requirements: Apple Macinosh II or Apple Macintosh SE or Apple
Macintosh Plus and a hard disk drive; or Apple Macintosh 512K Enhanced with 1
megabyte of memory and a hard disk drive; Apple System 4.1 and Finder 5.5 or
later; ImageWriter, color ImageWriter, or LaserWriter printer, or other
PostScript compatible device.
10 500       Title from title screen.
11 520       Formats pages of newsletters, newspapers, and documents for printing.
12 650   0  Desktop publishing.
13 700 10  Jaech, Jeremy.
14 710 20  Aldus Corporation.
15 753       Macintosh.
16 740 01  Pagemaker.
17 740 01  Page maker.
```

Example 12A

Title from disk label

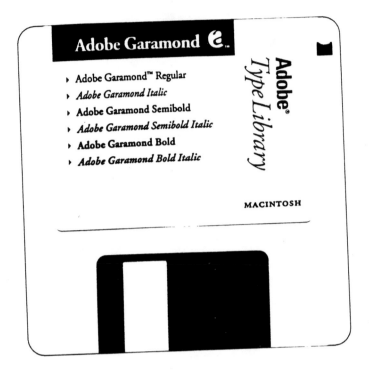

Title from "About" screen

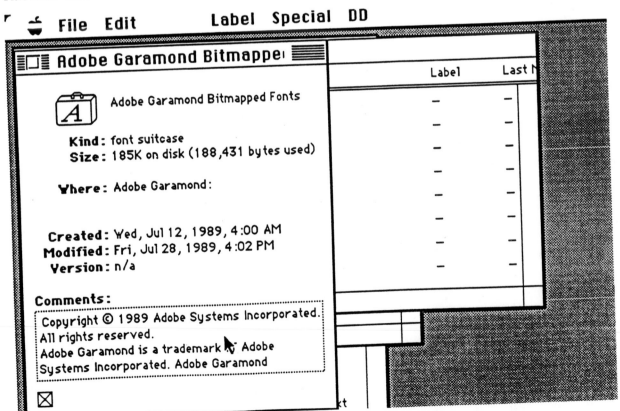

Example 12A

> Adobe Garamond [computer file]. -- Macintosh version. -- Mountain
> View, Calif. : Adobe Systems, 1990.
> 1 computer disk ; 3 1/2 in. + 1 user guide + 1 quick
> reference card + 1 sample character set chart. -- (Adobe type
> library)
>
> Electronic typefaces for use in desktop publishing.
> System requirements: Macintosh; 512K RAM; two 800K disk
> drives or one 800K disk drive with hard disk; PostScript output
> device.
> Title from disk label.
> Includes Adobe Garamond regular, italic, semibold, semibold
> italic, bold, and bold italic.
>
>
> 1. Type and type-founding--Computer programs. 2. Desktop
> publishing. I. Adobe Systems, Inc. II. Macintosh.
>
> Z286.D47

This pair of examples show cataloging of two different sets of type faces. The bibliographic records are identical except for the title proper and the informal contents note. The fonts carry a copyright date of 1989, but the manuals and packaging indicate this was published in 1990.
Rules for notes are 9.7B1a, 9.7B1b, 9.7B3, and 9.7B18.


```
Type: m      Bib lvl: m Source: d   Lang: eng
File: m      Enc lvl: I Govt pub:   Ctry: cau
Audience: f Mod rec:    Frequen: n Regulr:
Desc: a      Dat tp: s Dates: 1990,
 1 040
 2 090      XXX ǂc XXX
 3 090      Z286.D47
 4 049      XXXX
 5 245 00  Adobe Garamond ǂh computer file
 6 250      Macintosh version.
 7 260      Mountain View, Calif. : ǂb Adobe Systems, ǂc 1990.
 8 300      1 computer disk ; ǂc 3 1/2 in. + ǂe 1 user guide + 1 quick reference
card + 1 sample character set chart.
 9 440  0 Adobe type library
10 500      Electronic typefaces for use in desktop publishing.
11 538      System requirements: Macintosh; 512K RAM; two 800K disk drives or one
800K disk drive with hard disk; PostScript output device.
12 500      Title from disk label.
13 500      Includes Adobe Garamond regular, italic, semibold, semibold italic,
bold, and bold italic.
14 650  0 Type and type-founding ǂx Computer programs.
15 650  0 Desktop publishing.
16 710 20 Adobe Systems, Inc.
17 753      Macintosh.
```

Example 12B

Title from disk label

Title from "About" screen

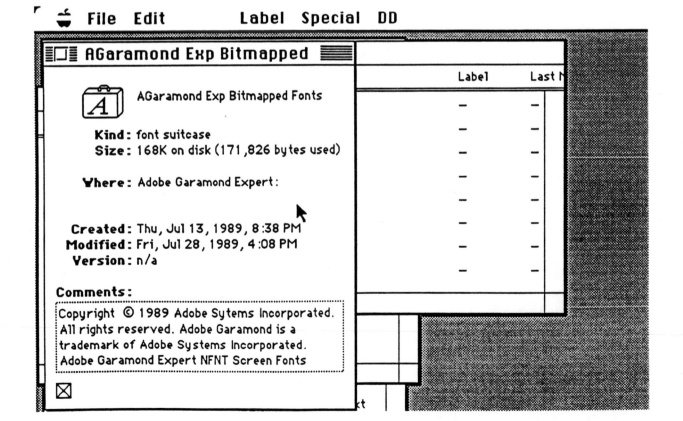

Example 12B

>
> Adobe Garamond expert collection [computer file]. -- Macintosh
>   version. -- Mountain View, Calif. : Adobe Systems, 1990.
>   1 computer disk ; 3 1/2 in. + 1 user guide + 1 quick
> reference card + 1 sample character set chart. -- (Adobe type
> library)
>
> Electronic typefaces for use in desktop publishing.
>   System requirements: Macintosh; 512K RAM; two 800K disk
> drives or one 800K disk drive with hard disk; PostScript output
> device.
>   Title from disk label.
>   Includes Adobe Garamond titling capitals, alternate regular,
> alternate italic, expert regular, expert italic, expert
> semibold, expert semibold italic, expert bold, and expert bold
> italic.
>
> 1. Type and type-founding--Computer programs. 2. Desktop
> publishing. I. Adobe Systems, Inc. II. Macintosh.
>
> Z286.D47

```
Type: m      Bib lvl: m Source: d   Lang: eng
File: m      Enc lvl: I Govt pub:   Ctry: cau
Audience: f Mod rec:   Frequen: n  Regulr:
Desc: a      Dat tp: s  Dates: 1990,
 1 040
 2 090     XXX ǂc XXX
 3 090     Z286.D47
 4 049     XXXX
 5 245 00  Adobe Garamond expert collection ǂh computer file
 6 250     Macintosh version.
 7 260     Mountain View, Calif. : ǂb Adobe Systems, ǂc 1990.
 8 300     1 computer disk ; ǂc 3 1/2 in. + ǂe 1 user guide + 1 quick reference
card + 1 sample character set chart.
 9 440  0 Adobe type library
10 500     Electronic typefaces for use in desktop publishing.
11 538     System requirements: Macintosh; 512K RAM; two 800K disk drives or one
800K disk drive with hard disk; PostScript output device.
12 500     Title from disk label.
13 500     Includes Adobe Garamond titling capitals, alternate regular,
alternate italic, expert regular, expert italic, expert semibold, expert
semibold italic, expert bold, and expert bold italic.
14 650  0 Type and type-founding ǂx Computer programs.
15 650  0 Desktop publishing.
16 710 20 Adobe Systems, Inc.
17 753     Macintosh.
```

50

Example 13

Title from title screen

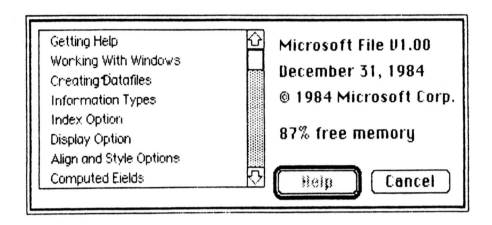

Example 13

```
Microsoft file [computer file] -- V[ersion] 1.00. -- Bellevue, WA
   : Microsoft Corp., c1984.
      1 computer disk ; 3 1/2 in. + 1 manual (246 p. : ill. ; 23
cm.)

      System requirements: Macintosh; 128K; printer and second
disk drive optional.
      Title from title screen.
      Summary: Designed to store, retrieve, and process
information and prepare reports.


      1. Data base management.  I. Microsoft Corporation.  II.
Macintosh.  III. Title: File.

   QA76.9.D3
```

The version number appeared on the title screen as V1.00. I chose to bracket in the rest of the word "version" to make this clearer.

The Library of Congress name authority file gives "Microsoft Corporation" as the form to be used in the added entry. Rules for notes are 9.7B1b, 9.7B3, 9.7B17.

```
Type: m      Bib lvl: m Source: d   Lang: eng
File: b      Enc lvl: I Govt pub:   Ctry: wau
Audience: f Mod rec:    Frequen: n  Regulr:
Desc: a      Dat tp: s  Dates: 1984,
 1 010
 2 040     XXX ǂc XXX
 3 090     QA76.9.D3
 4 049     XXXX
 5 245 00  Microsoft file ǂh computer file
 6 250     V[ersion] 1.00.
 7 260     Bellevue, WA : ǂb Microsoft Corp., ǂc c1984.
 8 300     1 computer disk ; ǂc 3 1/2 in. + ǂe 1 manual (246 p. : ill. ; 23cm.)
 9 538     System requirements: Macintosh; 128K; printer and second disk drive
optional.
10 500     Title from title screen.
11 520     Designed to store, retrieve, and process information and prepare
reports.
12 650  0  Data base management.
13 710 20  Microsoft Corporation.
14 753     Macintosh.
15 740 01  File.
```

Example 14

Title screens

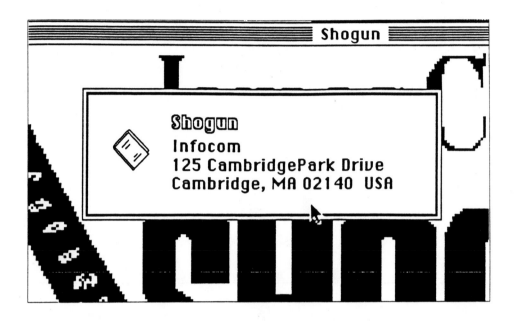

Example 14

    Shōgun [computer file] : a story of Japan. -- Release 292. --
        Cambridge, MA : Infocom ; distributed by Mediagenic, c1988.
            1 computer disk : col. ; 3 1/2 in. + 1 instruction manual +
        1 reference card + 1 map + 1 information sheet.

            Interactive fiction.
            System requirements: Macintosh (Mac II for color); 512K;
        hard disk or 2 disk drives; printer.
            Title from title screen. Title on container: James Clavell's
        Shōgun.
            Adapted by Dave Lebling.
            Based on: Shōgun / by James Clavell. London : Noble House
        Trading, c1975.
            "True to the original in its strong language, adult themes,
        and frank depictions of violence. It may not be appropriate for
        children"--Container.
            Also available for IBM and compatibles, Apple II series,
        Apple IIGS, Atari ST, and Amiga.
            Summary: User plays role of English seaman John Blackthorne,
        pilot-major of the Dutch trader-warship Erasmus, on a secret
        mission of trade and plunder to the Spanish-dominated Pacific
        Ocean in the year 1600. Shipwrecked on the coast of Japan,
        Blackthorne is thrust into the culture of ancient Japan.
            ISBN 0-87321-423-4.

            1. Japan--History--Tokugawa period, 1600-1868. 2. Computer
        games. I. Lebling, Dave. II. Clavell, James. Shōgun. III.
        Infocom, Inc. IV. Mediagenic. V. Title: James Clavell's
        Shōgun. VI. Macintosh.

        DS871.77

Notice the list of types of computers for which this game is available.
Rules for notes are, in order, 9.7B1a, 9.7B1b, 9.7B3, 9.7B6, 9.7B7, 9.7B14, 9.7B16, 9.7B17.


```
Type: m      Bib lvl: m Source: d   Lang: eng
File: b      Enc lvl: I Govt pub:   Ctry: mau
Audience:    Mod rec:   Frequen: n  Regulr:
Desc: a      Dat tp: s Dates: 1988,
 1 010
 2 040      XXX ǂc XXX
 3 020      0873214234
 4 090      DS871.77
 5 049      XXXX
 6 245 00  Sh⁻ogun ǂh computer file : ǂb a story of Japan.
 7 250      Release 292.
 8 260      Cambridge, MA : ǂb Infocom ; distributed by Mediagenic, ǂc c1988.
 9 300      1 computer disk : ǂb col. ; ǂc 3 1/2 in. + ǂe 1 instruction manual +
1 reference card + 1 map + 1 information sheet.
```
(Continued on next page)

10 500   Interactive fiction.
11 538   System requirements: Macintosh (Mac II for color); 512K; hard disk or 2 disk drives; printer.
12 500   Title from title screen. Title on container: James Clavell's Sh~ogun.
13 500   Adapted by Dave Lebling.
14 500   Based on: Sh~ogun / by James Clavell. London : Noble House Trading, c1975.
15 500   "True to the original in its strong language, adult themes, and frank depictions of violence. It may not be appropriate for children"--Container.
16 500   Also available for IBM and compatibles, Apple II series, Apple IIGS, Atari ST, and Amiga.
17 520   User plays role of English seaman John Blackthorne, pilot-major of the Dutch trader-warship Erasmus, on a secret mission of trade and plunder to the Spanish-dominated Pacific Ocean in the year 1600. Shipwrecked on the coast of Japan, Blackthorne is thrust into the culture of ancient Japan.
18 651 0 Japan ‡x History ‡y Tokugawa period, 1600-1868.
19 650 0 Computer games.
20 700 10 Lebling, Dave.
21 700 11 Clavell, James. ‡t Sh~ogun
22 710 20 Infocom, Inc.
23 710 20 Mediagenic.
24 740 01 James Clavell's Sh~ogun.
25 753   Macintosh.

Example 15

Title screen

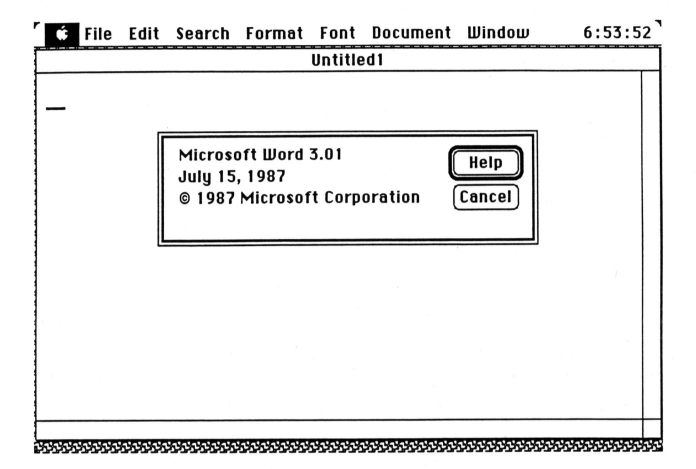

Example 15

```
Microsoft word [computer file]. -- Version 3.01. -- Redmond, WA :
    Microsoft Corp., c1987.
        2 computer disks ; 3 1/2 in. + 1 manual.

        Word processing program.
        System requirements: Macintosh; 512K; printer.
        Title from title screen.


        1. Word processing.  I. Microsoft Corporation.  II.
    Macintosh.  III. Title: Word.

    Z52.5.M4
```

This is a very brief record for a well-known computer program. It doesn't need any more detail. Rules for notes are 9.7B1a, 9.7B1b, 9.7B3.

```
Type: m       Bib lvl: m Source: d   Lang: eng
File: b       Enc lvl: I Govt pub:   Ctry: wau
Audience: f Mod rec:    Frequen: n Regulr:
Desc: a       Dat tp: s Dates: 1987,
 1 010
 2 040        XXX ‡c XXX
 3 090        Z52.5.M4
 4 049        XXXX
 5 245 00 Microsoft word ‡h computer file
 6 250        Version 3.01.
 7 260        Redmond, WA : ‡b Microsoft Corp., ‡c c1987.
 8 300        2 computer disks ; ‡c 3 1/2 in. + ‡e 1 manual.
 9 500        Word processing program.
10 538        System requirements: Macintosh; 512K; printer.
11 500        Title from title screen.
12 650    0 Word processing.
13 710 20 Microsoft Corporation.
14 753        Macintosh.
15 740 01 Word.
```

Example 15B

```
Microsoft word [computer file]. -- Version 3.01. -- Redmond, WA :
    Microsoft Corp., c1987.

        Word processing program.
        System requirements: Macintosh; 512K; printer.
        Available online through Mankato State University network.
        Title from title screen.


        1. Word processing.   I. Microsoft Corporation.   II.
    Macintosh.   III. Title: Word.
```

When the item is available online, there is no area 5. A note explains how the user is to get the computer file.

A call number would not be used.

58

Example 16

Title screens

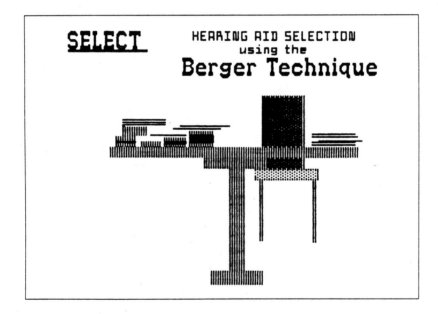

Example 16

```
Select.
     Parrot Software presents Select [computer file] : hearing aid
selection using the Berger technique. -- State College, PA :
Parrot Software, c1983.
     1 computer disk : sd. ; 5 1/4 in. + 1 manual (6 p. ; 22 cm.)

     System requirements: Apple II; optional program, Hearing aid
manager.
     Title from title screen.
     Manual: Select a hearing aid / Gary J. Glascoe.
     Summary: Uses the Berger technique to generate data needed to
 select the correct hearing aid from a number of specifications.


     1. Hearing aids--Fitting.  I. Glascoe, Gary J. Select a hearing
aid. 1983.  II. Parrot Software (Firm)  III. Apple II.


     RF300
```

This item has a "presents" title proper. In an LCRI for 7.1B1 (CSB 13) we are told to ignore this information in the case of motion pictures and videorecordings. We are not, however, to ignore it for other materials, but to transcribe the complete grammatically connected information as title proper. The "real" title is used as a uniform title main entry.
Rules for notes are 9.7B1b, 9.7B3, 9.7B11, 9.7B17.


```
Type: m     Bib lvl: m Source: d   Lang: eng
File: b     Enc lvl: I Govt pub:   Ctry: pau
Audience: f Mod rec:   Frequen: n  Regulr:
Desc: a     Dat tp: s  Dates: 1983,
 1 010
 2 040      XXX ‡c XXX
 3 090      RF300
 4 049      XXXX
 5 130 0    Select.
 6 245 00   Parrot Software presents Select ‡h computer file : ‡b hearing aid
selection using the Berger technique.
 7 260      State College, PA : ‡b Parrot Software, ‡c c1983.
 8 300      1 computer disk : ‡b sd. ; ‡c 5 1/4 in. + ‡e 1 manual (6 p. ; 22cm.)
 9 538      System requirements: Apple II; optional program, Hearing aid manager.
10 500      Title from title screen.
11 500      Manual: Select a hearing aid / Gary J. Glascoe.
12 520      Uses the Berger technique to generate data needed to select the
correct hearing aid from a number of specifications.
13 650  0   Hearing aids ‡x Fitting.
14 700 12   Glascoe, Gary J. ‡t Select a hearing aid. ‡f 1983.
15 710 20   Parrot Software (Firm)
16 753      Apple II.
```

60

Example 17

Title screen

```
MIDWEST SOFTWARE ASSOCIATES present  TM
═══════════════════════════WRITE AWAY
A WORD PROCESSING/COMMUNICATIONS SYSTEM
COPYRIGHT 1984 by DOUGLAS B. STINSON
                  217 VICTORY LANE
                  ST CHARLES, MO  63303
┌──────────────────────────────────────┐
│          ALL RIGHTS RESERVED          │
├──────────────────────────────────────┤
│ DUPLICATION FOR OTHER THAN SINGLE-     │
│ SYSTEM BACKUP PURPOSES IS EXPRESSLY    │
│ PROHIBITED.                            │
└──────────────────────────────────────┘
┌──────────────────────────────────────┐
│ ═══════WRITE AWAY is published by:     │
│ MIDWEST SOFTWARE ASSOCIATES            │
│     1160 APPLESEED LANE                │
│     ST. LOUIS, MO  63132               │
└──────────────────────────────────────┘
```

Examples 17

```
Stinson, Douglas B.
   [Write away]
   Midwest Software Associates present Write away [computer file]
: a word processing/communications system. -- St. Louis, MO :
Midwest Software Associates, c1984.
   1 computer disk ; 5 1/4 in. + 1 manual + 1 command card.

   System requirements: Apple II; 80 column card; modem; printer.
   Title from title screen.
   Copyright and manual by Douglas B. Stinson.


   1. Word processing.  I. Midwest Software Associates.  II.
Title: Write away.  III. Apple II.

Z52.5.W7
```

Stinson was chosen as main entry because he has the copyright on the software and is the author of the manual. One may consider him "chiefly responsible for the creation of the intellectual or artistic content of a work" as in rule 21.1, even though he is not named on the title screen. We may use information from the copyright statement in this fashion, but must include the information in a note, as shown above, rather than in the statement of responsibility.

A uniform title is made for the "real" title in this example, and that title is also traced with an added entry.

Rules for notes are 9.7B1b, 9.7B3, 9.7B6.

```
Type: m      Bib lvl: m Source: d   Lang: eng
File: b      Enc lvl: I Govt pub:   Ctry: mou
Audience: f Mod rec:   Frequen: n  Regulr:
Desc: a      Dat tp: s  Dates: 1984,
 1 010
 2 040     XXX ‡c XXX
 3 090     Z52.5.W7
 4 049     XXXX
 5 100 1   Stinson, Douglas B.
 6 240 10  Write away
 7 245 00  Midwest Software Associates present Write away ‡h computer file : ‡b
a word processing/communications system.
 8 260     St. Louis, MO : ‡b Midwest Software Associates, ‡c c1984.
 9 300     1 computer disk ; ‡c 5 1/4 in. + ‡e 1 manual + 1 command card.
10 538     System requirements: Apple II; 80 column card; modem; printer.
11 500     Title from title screen.
12 500     Copyright and manual by Douglas B. Stinson.
13 650  0  Word processing.
14 710 20  Midwest Software Associates.
15 740 01  Write away.
16 753     Apple II.
```

Example 18

Title screen

```
                   STONEWARE'S

           =>    DB MASTER    <=

                  (REV. 3.02!)

               SERIAL # 44267A


      (C) 1980. 1982 DB MASTER ASSOCIATES
          ALL RIGHTS RESERVED 2222

      PRESS 'RETURN' TO CONTINUE ...
```

Example 18

```
DB Master.
    Stoneware's DB master [computer file] -- Rev. 3.02. -- San
Rafael, Calif. : Stoneware, c1982.
    1 computer disk ; 5 1/4 in. + 1 manual.

    System requirements: Apple II+ or IIe; 2 disk drives; printer.
    Title from title screen.
    Summary: Allows creation, storage, manipulation, and
preparation of reports based upon input files.


    1. Data base management.   I. Stoneware Incorporated.   II.
Title: D B master.   III. Apple II+.   IV. Apple IIe.

    QA76.9.D3
```

Here we have a title proper that includes a possessive. This is transcribed as part of the title proper. A uniform title is used as main entry.

The added entry for the company uses the form of name found on the item itself. The company is not listed in LC's authority file.

Rules for notes are 9.7B1b, 9.7B3, 9.7B17.

```
Type: m      Bib lvl: m Source: d   Lang: eng
File: b      Enc lvl: I Govt pub:   Ctry: cau
Audience: f Mod rec:     Frequen: n  Regulr:
Desc: a       Dat tp: s  Dates: 1982,
 1 010
 2 040       XXX ǂc XXX
 3 090       QA76.9.D3
 4 049       XXXX
 5 130  0    DB master.
 6 245 10    Stoneware's DB master ǂh computer file
 7 250       Rev. 3.02.
 8 260       San Rafael, Calif. : ǂb Stoneware, ǂc c1982.
 9 300       1 computer disk ; ǂc 5 1/4 in. + ǂe 1 manual.
10 538       System requirements: Apple II+ or IIe; 2 disk drives; printer.
11 500       Title from title screen.
12 520       Allows creation, storage, manipulation, and preparation of reports
based upon input files.
13 650  0    Data base management.
14 710 20    Stoneware Incorporated.
15 740 01    D B master.
16 753       Apple II+.
17 753       Apple IIe.
```

64

Example 19A

Title screen

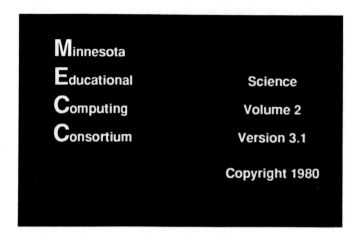

Science. Volume 2 [computer file] / Minnesota Educational
    Computing Corporation. -- Version 3.1. -- St. Paul, Minn. :
    MECC, c1980.
        1 computer disk ; 5 1/4 in. + 1 manual (84 p. : ill. ; 28
    cm.)

        System requirements: Apple II.
        Title from title screen.
        Contents: Cell membrane [simulation of interaction within
    cell] -- Collide [simulation, collision of two bodies, momentum
    and kinetic energy] -- Diffusion [simulation, relative
    diffusion rates of gases] -- ICBM [simulation, calculations for
    interception] -- Nuclear simulation [illustrates radioactive
    decay of 9 isotopes] -- Pest [simulation, interactions between
    pesticides and environment] -- Radar [educational game,
    interception of ICBM] -- Snell [simulation, refraction of light
    waves].

        I. Minnesota Educational Computing Corporation. II. Apple
    II. III. Title: Cell membrane. 1980. IV. Collide. 1980. V.
    Diffusion. 1980. VI. ICBM. 1980. VII. Nuclear simulation.
    1980. VIII. Pest. 1980. IX. Radar. 1980. X. Snell. 1980.

    Q182

Example 19A

A brief description is added to each title in the summary. The contents note contains information transcribed directly from the item; information added to this transcription must be bracketed. This technique is more efficient than constructing a separate summary for each of the programs involved.

I did not add subject headings to this example. It could have one, **Science**, or one or more subject headings for each program listed in the contents note.

Rules for notes are 9.7B1b, 9.7B3, 9.7B18.

```
Type: m      Bib lvl: m Source: d   Lang: eng
File: m      Enc lvl: I Govt pub:   Ctry: mnu
Audience: d Mod rec:    Frequen: n  Regulr:
Desc: a      Dat tp: s  Dates: 1980,
 1 010
 2 040     XXX ǂc XXX
 3 090     Q182
 4 049     XXXX
 5 245 00  Science. ǂn Volume 2 ǂh computer file / ǂc Minnesota Educational
Computing Corporation.
 6 250     Version 3.1.
 7 260     St. Paul, Minn. : ǂb MECC, ǂc c1980.
 8 300     1 computer disk ; ǂc 5 1/4 in. + ǂe 1 manual (84 p. : ill. ; 28 cm.)
 9 538     System requirements: Apple II.
10 500     Title from title screen.
11 505 0   Cell membrane [simulation of interaction within cell] -- Collide
[simulation, collision of two bodies, momentum and kinetic energy] -- Diffusion
[simulation, relative diffusion rates of gases] -- ICBM [simulation,
calculations for interception] -- Nuclear simulation [illustrates radioactive
decay of 9 isotopes] -- Pest [simulation, interactions between pesticides and
environment] -- Radar [educational game, interception of ICBM] -- Snell
[simulation, refraction of light waves].
12 710 20  Minnesota Educational Computing Corporation.
13 753 02  Apple II.
14 730 02  Cell membrane. ǂf 1980.
15 730 02  Collide. ǂf 1980.
16 730 02  Diffusion. ǂf 1980.
17 730 02  ICBM. ǂf 1980.
18 730 02  Nuclear simulation. ǂf 1980.
19 730 02  Pest. ǂf 1980.
20 730 02  Radar. ǂf 1980.
21 730 02  Snell. ǂf 1980.
```

Example 19B

From the manual

CELL MEMBRANE
  a simulation of the interaction between a cell and six factors in its
  internal and external environments.

COLLIDE
  a simulation of the collision of two bodies which displays the outcome
  in terms of momentum and kinetic energy.

DIFFUSION
  a simulation on the relative diffusion rates of gases.

ICBM
  a simulation of the interception of an ICBM which involves students in
  the underlying mathematical calculations.

NUCLEAR SIMULATION
  a simulation which illustrates the radioactive decay of nine different
  isotopes.

PEST
  a simulation of interactions which occur between pesticides and the
  environment.

RADAR
  an educational game which simulates the interception of an enemy
  ICBM.

SNELL
  a simulation of the refraction of light waves as they pass between two
  mediums.

Example 19B

```
Cell membrane [computer file].
      on 1 computer disk ; 5 1/4 in. + 1 guide (8 p. : ill. ; 28
cm.)

      In Science. Volume 2. -- Version 3.1. -- St. Paul, Minn. :
MECC, c1980.

      System requirements: Apple II.
      Title from title screen.
      Summary: Simulates the interaction between cell and its
environment. User controls six factors of the environment.


      1. Cell membranes.  2. Membranes (Biology)  I. Minnesota
Educational Computing Consortium.  II. Apple II.

      Q182
```

This is an example of an "in" analytic cataloged from the preceding example. We may choose to catalog selected contents in this manner as directed in rule 13.5 The "in" analytic part of the bibliographic description is as explained in rule 13.5A. It is coded as a field 773 in the MARC record shown below.

"Bib lvl" is coded "a" as a monographic component part of another item.

Rules for notes are 9.7B1b, 9.7B3, 9.7B17.

```
Type: m      Bib lvl: a Source: d   Lang: eng
File: m      Enc lvl: I Govt pub:   Ctry: mnu
Audience: d Mod rec:   Frequen: n  Regulr:
Desc: a      Dat tp: s  Dates: 1980,
 1 010
 2 040     XXX ǂc XXX
 3 090     Q182
 4 049     XXXX
 5 245 00  Cell membrane ǂh computer file
 6 300     on 1 computer disk ; ǂc 5 1/4 in. + ǂe 1 guide (8 p. : ill. ; 28cm.)
 7 538     System requirements: Apple II.
 8 500     Title from title screen.
 9 520     Simulates the interaction between cell and its environment. User
controls six factors of the environment.
10 650  0  Cell membrane.
11 650  0  Membranes (Biology)
12 710 20  Minnesota Educational Computing Consortium.
13 753     Apple II.
14 773 0   ǂ7 nnmm ǂt Science. Volume 2. ǂb Version 3.1. ǂd St. Paul, Minn. :
MECC, c1980. ǂw (OCoLC)nnnnnnn
```

68

Example 20A

Title screens

$$Bookends$$

© 1983
Jonathan D. Ashwell

SENSIBLE
SOFTWARE

```
        Bookends
The Reference Management System
       Copyright 1983
            by
     Jonathan D. Ashwell
   Sensible Software, Inc.
```

Example 20A

Ashwell, Jonathan D.
    Bookends [computer file] : the reference management system. --
Oak Park, Mich. : Sensible Software, c1983.
    1 computer disk ; 5 1/4 in. + 1 manual (79 p. ; 23 cm.)

    System requirements: Apple II; printer.
    Title from title screen.
    Copyright and manual by Jonathan D. Ashwell.
    Summary: Designed to save, retrieve, and format references, and
to print bibliographies.

    1. Information storage and retrieval systems. 2. Bibliographic
citations--Computer programs. I. Sensible Software, Inc. II.
Apple II. III. Title. IV. Title: Bookends, the reference
management system.

    Z1001

These two examples show the cataloging of two editions of a program. The new version has disks for each of the two sizes of Apple disk drives. The added entry for the company uses the form shown because that is the form of name used by the company on the item (24.5C1, B.2).
    Rules for notes are 9.7B1b, 9.7B3, 9.7B6, 9.7B17.

Type: m   Bib lvl: m Source: d   Lang: eng
File: b   Enc lvl: I Govt pub: Ctry: miu
Audience: f Mod rec: Frequen: n Regulr:
Desc: a   Dat tp: s Dates: 1983,
 1 010
 2 040   XXX ǂc XXX
 3 090   Z1001
 4 049   XXXX
 5 100 1   Ashwell, Jonathan D.
 6 245 10   Bookends ǂh computer file : ǂb the reference management system.
 7 260   Oak Park, Mich. : ǂb Sensible Software, ǂc c1983.
 8 300   1 computer disk ; ǂc 5 1/4 in. + ǂe 1 manual (79 p. ; 23 cm.)
 9 538   System requirements: Apple II; printer.
10 500   Title from title screen.
11 500   Copyright and manual by Jonathan D. Ashwell.
12 520   Designed to save, retrieve, and format references, and to print
bibliographies.
13 650 0   Information storage and retrieval systems.
14 650 0   Bibliographic citations ǂx Computer program.
15 710 20   Sensible Software, Inc.
16 753   Apple II.
17 740 01   Bookends, the reference management system.

70

Example 20B

Title screen

```
------------------------------------
          BOOKENDS Extended
------------------------------------

     The Reference Management System

          Copyright 1983-1985

                   by

          Jonathan D. Ashwell

          Sensible Software, Inc.
```

Disk label

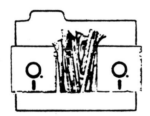

Bookends™
Extended

Sensible Software, Inc.®
© 1985 Jonathan D. Ashwell
© 1983 Apple Computer, Inc.

Example 20B

```
Ashwell, Jonathan D.
    Bookends extended [computer file] : the reference management
system. -- V2.08. -- Computer program. -- Birmingham, Mich. :
Sensible Software, c1985.
    2 computer disks ; 3 1/2-5 1/4 in. + 1 manual (107 p. ; 23 cm.)

    System requirements: Apple IIc or Apple IIe with 80 column
card; 128K; ProDOS; printer.
    Title from title screen.
    Copyright and manual by Jonathan D. Ashwell.
    Updated version of: Bookends.
    Summary: Designed to save, retrieve, and format references, and
to print bibliographies.


    1. Information storage and retrieval systems.  2. Bibliographic
citations--Computer programs.  I. Sensible Software, Inc.  II.
Bookends.  III. Apple IIe.  IV. Apple IIc.  V. Title.

    Z1001
```

Rules for notes are 9.7B1b, 9.7B3, 9.7B6, 9.7B7, 9.7B17.

```
Type: m      Bib lvl: m Source: d    Lang: eng
File: b      Enc lvl: I Govt pub:    Ctry: miu
Audience: f Mod rec:    Frequen: n  Regulr:
Desc: a      Dat tp: s  Dates: 1985,
 1 010
 2 040      XXX ‡c XXX
 3 090      Z1001
 4 049      XXXX
 5 100 1    Ashwell, Jonathan D.
 6 245 10   Bookends extended ‡h computer file : ‡b the reference management
system.
 7 250      V2.08.
 8 256      Computer program.
 9 260      Birmingham, Mich. : ‡b Sensible Software, ‡c c1985.
10 300      2 computer disks ; ‡c 3 1/2-5 1/4 in. + ‡e 1 manual (107 p. ; 23 cm.)
11 538      System requirements: Apple IIc or Apple IIe with 80 column card;
128K; ProDOS; printer.
12 500      Title from title screen.
13 500      Copyright and manual by Jonathan D. Ashwell.
14 500      Updated version of: Bookends.
15 520      Designed to save, retrieve, and format references, and to print
bibliographies.
16 650  0   Information storage and retrieval systems.
17 650  0   Bibliographic citations ‡x Computer programs.
18 710 20   Sensible Software, Inc.
19 730 01   Bookends.
20 753      Apple IIe.
21 753      Apple IIc.
```

72

Example 21A

Title screen

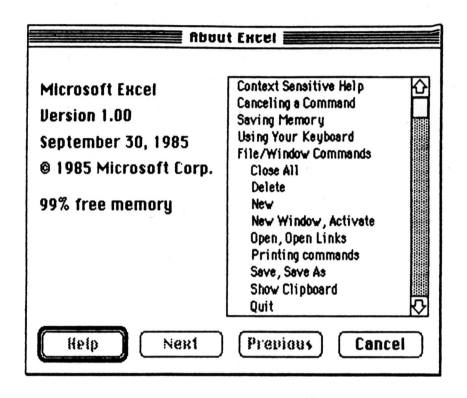

Example 21A

> Microsoft excel [computer file]. -- Version 1.00. -- Bellevue, WA
> : Microsoft Corp., c1985.
>   2 computer disks : 3 1/2 in. + 1 manual (365 p. : ill. ; 24
> cm.) + 1 quick reference guide (20 p. : ill. ; 18 cm.) + 1 manual
> (207 p. : ill. ; 22 cm.)
>
>   "Complete spreadsheet program with business graphics and
> database"--Manual.
>   System requirements: Macintosh; 512K; 2 disk drives; printer
> optional.
>   Title from title screen.
>   Title of second manual: Arrays, functions, and macros.
>   With: Hertzfeld, Andy. Switcher.
>
>
>   1. Electronic spreadsheets (Computer programs) I. Microsoft
> Corporation. II. Arrays, functions, and macros. 1985. III.
> Title: Excel. IV. Macintosh.
>
> HF5548.4

These two examples show "with" cataloging (1.17B21). The two items come together, but there is no collective title. Rules for notes are 9.7B1a, 9.7B1b, 9.7B3, 9.7B11, 9.7B21.

```
Type: m       Bib lvl: m Source: d   Lang: eng
File: b       Enc lvl: I Govt pub:   Ctry: wau
Audience: f Mod rec:    Frequen: n  Regulr:
Desc: a       Dat tp: s  Dates: 1985,
 1 010
 2 040     XXX ǂc XXX
 3 090     HF5548.4
 4 049     XXXX
 5 245 00  Microsoft excel ǂh computer file
 6 250     Version 1.00.
 7 260     Bellevue, WA : ǂb Microsoft Corp., ǂc c1985.
 8 300     2 computer disks ; ǂc 3 1/2 in. + ǂe 1 manual (365 p. : ill. ; 24cm.)
+ 1 quick reference guide (20 p. : ill. ; 18 cm.) + 1 manual (207 p. :ill. ; 22
cm.)
 9 500     "Complete spreadsheet program with business graphics and database"--
Manual.
10 538     System requirements: Macintosh; 512K; 2 disk drives; printer
optional.
11 500     Title from title screen.
12 500     Title of second manual: Arrays, functions, and macros.
13 501     With: Hertzfeld, Andy. Switcher.
14 650  0  Electronic spreadsheets (Computer program)
15 710 20  Microsoft Corporation.
16 730 02  Arrays, functions, and macros. ǂf 1985.
17 740 01  Excel.
18 753     Macintosh.
```

Example 21B

Title screen

 # Switcher
by Andy Hertzfeld

Version 4.4 -- August 12, 1985
© 1985 Apple Computer, Inc.

<u>Helpful Hints:</u>

Use ⌘[and ⌘] to rotate between applications.
Use ⌘\ to return back to the switcher.
Use the option key to transport the clipboard between applications (or not).
Use ⌘-shift-option-period as an "emergency exit" to exit hung applications.
The Finder can be run under the Switcher; open Switcher to quit from the Finder.
Click on the screen of the Mac icon to toggle saving screen bits to save 22K.

Thanks to John Markoff and Bud Tribble.

Example 21B

Hertzfeld, Andy.
    Switcher [computer file] / by Andy Hertzfeld. -- Cupertino,
Calif. : Apple Computer, c1985.
    on 1 computer disk : 3 1/2 in. + 1 manual (21 p. : ill. ; 22
cm.)

    System requirements: Macintosh; 512K.
    Title from title screen.
    Manual: Using Switcher with Microsoft applications. Bellevue,
WA : Microsoft Corp., c1984.
    Summary: Turns Macintosh into a multi-program workstation.
Allows user to have up to 8 programs in memory and switch between
them and share information.
    With: Microsoft excel.

    1. Utilities (Computer programs) I. Apple Computer, Inc.   II.
Microsoft Corporation. III. Using Switcher with Microsoft
applications. 1984. IV. Title. V. Macintosh.

    HF5548.4

Rules for notes are 9.7B1b, 9.7B3, 9.7B11, 9.7B17, 9.7B21.

Type: m   Bib lvl: m Source: d   Lang: eng
File: b   Enc lvl: I Govt pub: Ctry: cau
Audience: f Mod rec: Frequen: n Regulr:
Desc: a   Dat tp: s Dates: 1985,
 1 010
 2 040   XXX ‡c XXX
 3 090   HF5548.4
 4 049   XXXX
 5 100 1   Hertzfeld, Andy.
 6 245 10 Switcher ‡h computer file / ‡c by Andy Hertzfeld.
 7 260   Cupertino, Calif. : ‡b Apple Computer, ‡c c1985.
 8 300   on 1 computer disk ; ‡c 3 1/2 in. + ‡e 1 manual (21 p. : ill. ; 22
cm.)
 9 538   System requirements: Macintosh; 512K.
10 500   Title from title screen.
11 500   Manual: Using Switcher with Microsoft applications. Bellevue, WA :
Microsoft Corp., c1984.
12 520   Turns Macintosh into a multi-program workstation. Allows user to have
up to 8 programs in memory and switch between them and share information.
13 501   With: Microsoft excel.
14 650 0 Utilities (Computer programs)
15 710 20 Apple Computer, Inc.
16 710 20 Microsoft.
17 730 01 Using Switcher with Microsoft applications. ‡f 1984.
18 753   Macintosh.

Example 22

Title screen

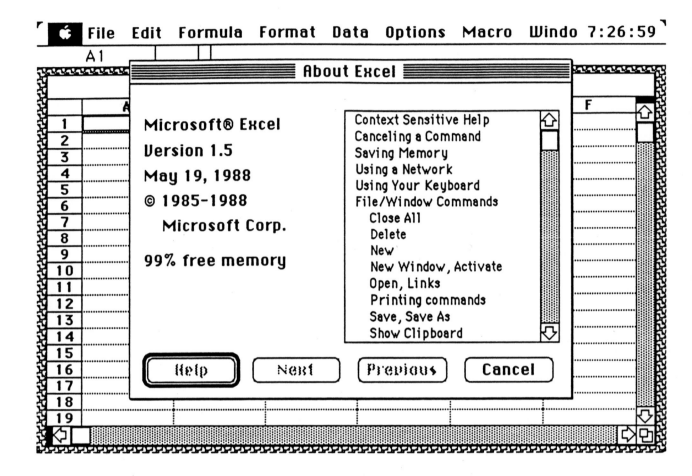

File   Edit   Formula   Format   Data   Options   Macro   Windo 7:26:59

A1

About Excel

Microsoft® Excel

Version 1.5

May 19, 1988

© 1985-1988

   Microsoft Corp.

99% free memory

Context Sensitive Help
Canceling a Command
Saving Memory
Using a Network
Using Your Keyboard
File/Window Commands
   Close All
   Delete
   New
   New Window, Activate
   Open, Links
   Printing commands
   Save, Save As
   Show Clipboard

Help   Next   Previous   Cancel

Example 22

```
Microsoft excel [computer file]. -- Version 1.5. -- Redmond, WA :
    Microsoft Corp., 1988.
        1 computer disk : col. ; 3 1/2 in. + 2 manuals.

    "Complete spreadsheet program with business graphics and
database."--Manual.
        System requirements: Macintosh 512KE, Plus, SE, or II;
System 3.2 and Finder 5.3 or later; printer.
        Title from title screen.


        1. Electronic spreadsheets (Computer programs)  I. Microsoft
Corporation.  II. Macintosh.  III. Title: Excel.

        HF5548.4
```

The program Switcher does not come with version 1.5 of this program as it did in the previous example. Rules for notes are 9.7B1a, 9.7B1b, 9.7B3.

```
Type: m      Bib lvl: m Source: d    Lang: eng
File: b      Enc lvl: I Govt pub:    Ctry: wau
Audience: f Mod rec:    Frequen: n  Regulr:
Desc: a      Dat tp: s  Dates: 1988,
 1 010
 2 040      XXX ‡c XXX
 3 090      HF5548.4
 4 049      XXXX
 5 245 00  Microsoft excel ‡h computer file
 6 250      Version 1.5.
 7 260      Redmond, WA : ‡b Microsoft Corp., ‡c c1988.
 8 300      1 computer disk ‡b col. ; ‡c 3 1/2 in. + ‡e 2 manuals
 9 500      "Complete spreadsheet program with business graphics and database"--
Manual.
10 538      System requirements: Macintosh 512KE, Plus, SE or II; System 3.2 and
Finder 5.3 or later; printer.
11 500      Title from title screen.
12 650   0  Electronic spreadsheets (Computer programs)
13 710 20  Microsoft Corporation.
14 753      Macintosh.
15 740 01  Excel.
```

Example 23

Verso title page of manual

Printing History

Nolo Press is committed to keeping its books up-to-date. Each new print-ing, whether or not it is called a new edition, has been completely revised to reflect the latest law changes. This book was printed and updated on the last date indicated below. Before you rely on information in it, you might wish to call Nolo Press (415) 549-1976 to check whether a later printing or edition has been issued.

New "**Printing**" means there have been some minor changes, but usually not enough so that people will need to trade in or discard an earlier printing of the same edition. Obviously, this is a judgment call and any change, no matter how minor, might affect you. New "**Edition**" means one or more major, or a number of minor, law changes since the previous edition.

License Information

WillMaker is sold solely for the private noncommercial use of its purchasers. It is a violation of United States copyright law to duplicate the WillMaker disc (except for the backup copy).

First Edition (1.0)	September 1985
Second Edition (2.0)	April 1986
Second Printing	August 1986
Third Printing	October 1986
Fourth Printing	May 1987
Fifth Printing	November 1987
Third Edition (3.0)	April 1988
Second Printing	June 1988
Third Printing	March 1989
WillMaker Program	Legisoft (Jeff Scargle & Bob Bergstrom)
WillMaker Manual	Nolo Press (Stephen Elias & Jake Warner)
Illustrations	Mari Stein
Production	Stephanie Harolde & Glenn Voloshin
Book Design	Keija Kimura
Packaging Design	Carol Pladsen
Index	Sayre Van Young

ISBN 0-87337-107-0 (IBM 3 1/2)
ISBN 0-87337-063-5 (IBM 5 1/4)
ISBN 0-87337-065-1 (Macintosh)
ISBN 0-87337-064-3 (Apple)
Library of Congress Card Catalog No. 84-63151
© Copyright 1985, 1986 and 1988 by Nolo Press

Example 23

Title screens

```
*******************************************
                 WILL MAKER
*******************************************

   PUBLISHED BY:       NOLO PRESS
                       950 PARKER STREET
                       BERKELEY, CA 94710

       (C) Copyright 1985 by LEGISOFT INC.
       > LOADING PROGRAM...PLEASE WAIT <
```

```
             Welcome to WILLMAKER

        ...a program to help you write a
           simple but effective will.

           USING WILLMAKER YOU CAN:

     >  give property to your spouse,
        children, domestic partner, to
        charity, or anyone else

     >  set up a trust for your children

             AND YOU CAN NAME:

     >  a guardian for minor children

     >  a personal representative (execu-
        tor)
```

Example 23

```
Will maker [computer file]. -- [Version] 3.0. -- Berkeley, CA :
    Nolo Press, c1988.
        1 computer disk ; 3 1/2 in. + 1 manual (various pagings :
    ill. ; 24 cm.)

        "Use your computer to prepare & update your own valid will"
    --Cover of manual.
        System requirements: Macintosh 512K or higher; printer.
        Title from title screen.
        WillMaker program by Legisoft; WillMaker manual by Nolo
    Press.
        Previous title: WillWriter.


        1. Wills--United States--Software.  I. Nolo Press.  II.
    Legisoft (Firm)  III. WillWriter.  IV. Title: WillMaker.  V.
    Macintosh.

    KF755
```

The title is done as one word most places, however, it is two words on the first title screen.
Rules for notes are 9.7B1a, 9.7B1b, 9.7B3, 9.7B6, 9.7B7.

```
Type: m      Bib lvl: m Source: d  Lang: eng
File: m      Enc lvl: I Govt pub:  Ctry: cau
Audience: f Mod rec:    Frequen: n Regulr:
Desc: a      Dat tp: s  Dates: 1988,
 1 010
 2 020      0873370651
 3 040      XXX ‡c XXX
 4 090      KF5755
 5 049      XXXX
 6 245 00   Will maker ‡h computer file
 7 250      [Version] 3.0.
 8 260      Berkeley, CA : ‡b Nolo Press, ‡c c1988.
 9 300      1 computer disk ; ‡c 3 1/2 in. + ‡e 1 manual (various pagings : ill.
; 24 cm.)
10 500      "Use your computer to prepare & update your own valid will"--Cover of
manual.
11 538      System requirements: Macintosh 512K or higher; printer.
12 500      Title from title screen.
13 500      Previous title: WillWriter.
14 650   0  Wills ‡z United States ‡x Software.
15 710 20   Nolo Press.
16 730 20   Legisoft (Firm)
17 730 01   WillWriter.
18 740 01   WillMaker.
19 753      Macintosh.
```

Example 24

Title screen

```
*** dBASE II/86   Ver 2.41A  1 June 1984

COPYRIGHT (c) ASHTON-TATE 1984
AS AN UNPUBLISHED LICENSED PROPRIETARY WORK.
ALL RIGHTS RESERVED.

Use of this software has been provided under a Soft-
ware License Agreement (please read in full).  In
summary, you may produce only three back-up copies and
use this software only on a single computer and single
terminal.  You may not grant sublicenses nor transfer
the software or related materials in any form to any
person unless Ashton-Tate consents in writing.  This
software contains valuable trade secrets and propri-
etary information, and is protected by federal copy-
right laws, the violation of which can result in civil
damages and criminal prosecution.

dBASE II is a registered trademark and dBASE and
ASHTON-TATE are trademarks of Ashton-Tate.

           This is a restricted educational version
               of dBASE II(TM) from Ashton-Tate
                      as part of the
                  IBM APPRENTICE PROGRAM
                   by Prentice-Hall
```

Example 24

From the manual

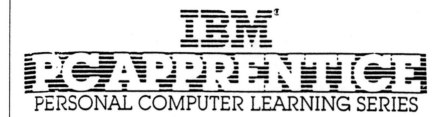

PERSONAL COMPUTER LEARNING SERIES

ASHTON·TATE™

Deborah Stone

A PRENTICE-HALL/CHAMBERS TUTORIAL WORKBOOK

PRENTICE-HALL, INC., Englewood Cliffs, N.J. 07632

Example 24

```
    dBASE II [computer file]. -- Ver[sion] 2.41A. -- Englewood Cliffs,
        N.J. : Prentice-Hall, c1984.
            1 computer disk ; 5 1/4 in. + 1 workbook (231 p. : ill. ; 24
        cm.) -- (IBM PC apprentice personal computer learning series)

            System requirements: IBM PC; printer.
            Title from title screen.
            Software copyright: Ashton-Tate.
            Workbook by Deborah Stone.
            Summary: Tutorial on use of computer program, dBASE II.


            1. dBase II (Computer program)--Study and teaching.  I.
        Stone, Deborah.  II. Prentice-Hall, Inc.  III. Ashton-Tate
        (Firm)  IV. IBM PC.  V. Series.

        QA76.9.D3
```

This is cataloged as a computer disk accompanied by a thick workbook. It could just as well be considered to be a book accompanied by a disk (or a kit).

The subject heading is coded as field 630, uniform title.

Rules for notes are 9.7B1b, 9.7B3, 9.7B6, 9.7B6, 9.7B17.

```
Type: m      Bib lvl: m Source: d   Lang: eng
File: b      Enc lvl: I Govt pub:   Ctry: nju
Audience: f Mod rec:    Frequen: n  Regulr:
Desc: a      Dat tp: s  Dates: 1984,
 1 010
 2 040      XXX ǂc XXX
 3 090      QA76.9.D3
 4 049      XXXX
 5 245 00   dBASE II ǂh computer file
 6 250      Ver[sion] 2.41A.
 7 260      Englewood Cliffs, N.J. : ǂb Prentice-Hall, ǂc c1984.
 8 300      1 computer disk ; ǂc 5 1/4 in. + ǂe 1 workbook (231 p. : ill. ; 24
cm.)
 9 440   0  IBM PC apprentice personal computer learning series
10 538      System requirements: IBM PC; printer.
11 500      Title from title screen.
12 500      Software copyright: Ashton-Tate.
13 500      Workbook by Deborah Stone.
14 520      Tutorial on use of computer program, dBASE II.
15 630 00   dBase II (Computer program) ǂx Study and teaching.
16 700 10   Stone, Deborah.
17 710 21   Prentice-Hall, Inc.
18 710 21   Ashton-Tate (Firm)
19 753      IBM-PC.
```

84

Example 25

Manual title page

The Power® Of:
Construction Management Using Lotus 1-2-3™

by Jay C. Compton

Edited by:
Estelle Phillips
Theresa Simone

Management Information Source, Inc.

Verso title page

Disk label

The Power Of	CONSTRUCTION MANAGEMENT USING LOTUS 1-2-3		
	FILE NAMES:		
	EquipCos	BidUnit1	ECosting
Professional Series	HaulUnit	BidUnit2	JCosting
	EstUnit	BidLump1	PaySched
	EstLump	BidLump2	CashMan

Title screen

```
The IBM Personal Computer DOS
Version 2.10 (c) Copyright IBM Corp 1981, 1982, 1983
```

Example 25

```
Compton, Jay C.
    The power of construction management using Lotus 1-2-3 / by Jay
C. Compton ; edited by Estelle Phillips, Theresa Simone. --
Portland, Or. : Management Information Source, c1984.
    v, 300 p. : ill. ; 28 cm. + 1 computer disk. -- (The power of
professional series)

    System requirements: IBM PC; Lotus 1-2-3 computer program.
    "Disk contains worksheets with labels and formulas already
entered"--Instructions.
    ISBN 0-943518-17-2.

    1. Construction industry--Management.  2. Lotus 1-2-3 (Computer
program)  I. Phillips, Estelle, 1928-     II. Simone, Theresa.
III. Management Information Source, Inc.  IV.  Title.  V. Title:
Construction management using Lotus 1-2-3.


TH437
```

In this example, the disk is considered to be accompanying material for the text, rather than the dominant item, so this package is cataloged as a book accompanied by a computer disk rather than as a computer disk accompanied by a book. The disk includes material that is printed in the book.

Rules for notes are 9.7B1b, 2.7B11.

```
Type: a Bib lvl: m Source: d   Lang: eng
Repr:    Enc lvl: I Conf pub: 0 Ctry: oru
Indx: 0 Mod rec:   Govt pub:   Cont:
Desc: a Int lvl:   Festschr: 0 Illus: a
F/B: 1  Dat tp: s  Dates: 1984,
 1 010
 2 040      XXX ‡c XXX
 3 020      0943518172
 4 090      TH437
 5 049      XXXX
 6 100 10   Compton, Jay C.
 7 245 14   The power of construction managment using Lotus 1-2-3 / ‡c by Jay C.Compton
; edited by Estelle Phillips, Theresa Simone.
 8 260 0    Portland, Or. : ‡b Management Information Source, ‡c c1984.
 9 300      v, 300 p. : ‡b ill. ; ‡c 28 cm. ‡e + 1 computer disk.
10 440   4  The power of professional series.
11 500      System requirements: IBM PC; Lotus 1-2-3 computer program.
12 500      "Disk contains worksheets with labels and formulas already entered"--
Instructions.
13 650   0  Construction industry ‡x Management.
14 700 10   Phillips, Estelle, ‡d 1928-
15 700 10   Simone, Theresa.
16 710 20   Management Information Source, Inc.
17 740 01   Construction management using Lotus 1-2-3.
```

Example 26

Title screens

A genealogical database HyperCard program
for the Macintosh computer

Distributed by the

Seattle Genealogical Society

P. O. Box 549

Seattle, WA 98111

Table of Contents

About MacAncestors

MacAncestors was developed for the Seattle Genealogical Society by
William H. "Bill" Blue and is being sold by the Society to raise funds
for the Society's Macintosh SE desktop publishing system. Neither the
Society nor the developer is responsible for the results of its use.
The developer will be happy to answer questions from registered
users on the use of MacAncestors by mail (SASE please), but please
study this manual first, especially the Addendum - Pitfalls to Avoid.
If your problem appears complex, send me a copy of your disk
containing all MacAncestors stacks.

Bill Blue
c/o Seattle Genealogical Society
P. O. Box 549
Seattle, WA 98111

MacAncestors Version 1.0
© 1988 Seattle Genealogical Society

 Table of Contents

Example 26

```
Blue, William H.
    MacAncestors [computer file]. -- Version 1.0. -- Seattle, WA :
Distributed by the Seattle Genealogical Society, c1988.
    1 computer disk ; 3 1/2 in.

    "A genealogical database HyperCard program for the Macintosh
computer."
    System requirements: Macintosh; HyperCard; hard disk; printer.
    Title from title screen.
    "Developed for the Seattle Genealogical Society by William H.
'Bill' Blue."


    1. Genealogy.  I. Seattle Genealogical Society.  II. Title.

CS24
```

Rules for notes are 9.7B1a, 9.7B1b, 9.7B3, 9.7B6.

```
Type: m      Bib lvl: m Source: d  Lang: eng
File: b      Enc lvl: I Govt pub:  Ctry: wau
Audience: f Mod rec:    Frequen: n Regulr:
Desc: a      Dat tp: s Dates: 1988,
 1 010
 2 040       XXX ǂc XXX
 3 090       CS24
 4 049       XXXX
 5 100 1     Blue, William H.
 6 245 10    MacAncestors ǂh computer file
 7 250       Version 1.0.
 8 260       Seattle, WA : ǂb Distributed by the Seattle Genealogical Society, ǂc
c1988.
 9 300       1 computer disk ; ǂc 3 1/2 in.
10 500       "A genealogical database HyperCard program for the Macintosh
computer."
11 538       System requirements: Macintosh; HyperCard; hard disk; printer.
12 500       Title from title screen.
13 500       "Developed for the Seattle Genealogical Society by William H. 'Bill'
Blue."
14 650  0    Genealogy.
15 710 20    Seattle Genealogical Society.
16 753       Macintosh.
```

88

Example 27

Cover of compact disk box

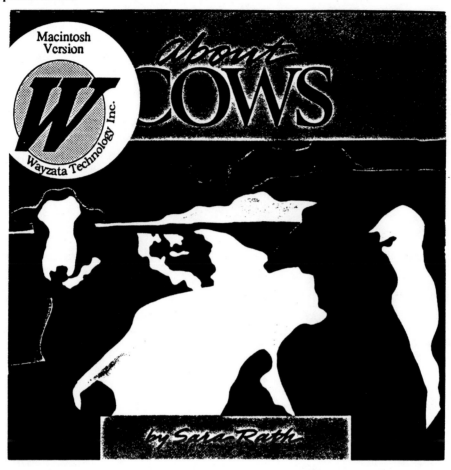

Computer disk label

Example 27

```
About cows [computer file] : by Sara Rath. -- Macintosh version,
    version 3.02. -- Grand Rapids, MN : Wayzata Technology, c1990.
        2 computer disks : sd., col. ; 3 1/2-4 3/4 in.

        System requirements: Macintosh; CD-ROM drive.
        Title from container.
        Based on: About cows / by Sara Rath. Ashland, WI : Heartland
    Press, c1987.
        Summary: Allows full-text search and retrieval of contents
    of book.


        1. Cows.  I. Rath, Sara. About cows.  III. Wayzata
    Technology Inc.  III. Macintosh.

        SF208
```

This computer program is not by Sara Rath. The book that is stored on the computer disk for searching is by Sara Rath. The cover of the package reproduced here is a copy of the book cover.

The version information used in area 2 is a combination of "Macintosh version" from a label stuck on the container, and "version 3.02" from the disk label.

Rules for notes are 9.7B1b, 9.7B3, 9.7B7, 9.7B17.

```
Type: m      Bib lvl: m Source: d   Lang: eng
File: m      Enc lvl: I Govt pub:   Ctry: mnu
Audience: f Mod rec:    Frequen: n  Regulr:
Desc: a      Dat tp: s  Dates: 1990,
 1 010
 2 040      XXX ‡c XXX
 3 090      SF208
 4 049      XXXX
 5 245 10   About cows ‡h computer file : ‡b by Sara Rath.
 6 250      Macintosh version, version 3.02.
 7 260      Grand Rapids, MN : ‡b Wayzata Technology, ‡c c1990.
 8 300      2 computer disks : ‡b sd., col. ; ‡c 3 1/2-4 3/4 in.
 9 538      System requirements: Macintosh; CD-ROM drive.
10 500      Title from container.
11 500      Based on: About cows / by Sara Rath.  Ashland, WI : Heartland Press,
c1987.
12 520      Allows full-text search and retrieval of contents of book.
13 650  0   Cows.
14 700 11   Rath, Sara. ‡t About cows.
15 710 20   Wayzata Technology Inc.
16 753      Macintosh.
```

90

Example 28

Printed side of compact disk

Example 28

```
Macworld superstacks! [computer file] : winners showcase. -- San
    Francisco, CA : Macworld Communications, c1990.
        1 computer disk : sd., col. ; 4 3/4 in.

        System requirements: Macintosh Plus; System 4.1; Finder 5.5;
    Apple CD SC or compatible drive.
        Title from disk label.
        Contents:  1. SuperStacks winners showcase [28 winning
    stacks from Macworld's 1989 contest] -- 2. Macworld interactive
    [full-color interactive presentation] -- 3. HyperCard 2.0 -- 4.
    HyperCard history [versions 1.0.1, 1.1, 1.2, 1.2.1, 1.2.2,
    1.2.5] -- 5. HyperCard international [Australian, Danish,
    Dutch, Finnish, Flemish, French, French-Canadian, French-Swiss,
    German-Swiss, Italian, Japanese (Kenji), Norwegian, and
    Swedish].


        1. HyperCard (Computer program)  2. Macintosh (Computer)--
    Programming.  I. HyperCard (Computer program). 1990.  II.
    Title: Superstacks!  III. Macworld Communications, Inc.  IV.
    Title: Winners showcase.  V. Macintosh Plus.

    QA76.8.M3
```

I wasn't sure what to use as title proper because the layout of words is confusing. I made a title added entry for the phrase I used as other title information.

The contents note combines contents and summary information as in example 19A.

Rules for notes are 9.7B1b, 9.7B3, 9.7B18.

```
Type: m      Bib lvl: m Source: d   Lang: eng
File: m      Enc lvl: I Govt pub:   Ctry: cau
Audience: f Mod rec:    Frequen: n  Regulr:
Desc: a      Dat tp: s  Dates: 1990,
 1 010
 2 040      XXX ‡c XXX
 3 090      QA76.8.M3
 4 049      XXXX
 5 245 00   Macworld superstacks! ‡h computer file : ‡b winners showcase
 6 260      San Francisco, CA : ‡b Macworld Communications, ‡c c1990.
 7 300      1 computer disk : ‡b sd., col. ; ‡c 4 3/4 in.
 8 538      System requirements: Macintosh Plus; System 4.1; Finder 5.5; Apple CD
SC or compatible drive.
 9 500      Title from disk label.
10 505 0    1. Super Stacks winners showcase [28 winning stacks from Macworld's
1989 contest] -- 2. Macworld interactive [full-color interactive presentation]
-- 3. HyperCard 2.0 -- 4. HyperCard history [versions 1.0.1, 1.1, 1.2, 1.2.1,
1.2.2, 1.2.5] -- 5. HyperCard international [Australian, Danish, Dutch, Finnish,
Flemish, French, French-Canadian, French-Swiss, German-Swiss, Italian, Japanese
(Kenji), Norwegian, and Swedish].
11 630 00 HyperCard (Computer program)
```
(Continued on next page)

```
12 650  0  Macintosh (Computer) ‡x Programming.
13 730 02  HyperCard (Computer program). ‡f 1990.
14 710 20  Macworld Communications, Inc.
15 740 01  Superstacks!
16 740 01  Winners showcase.
17 753     Macintosh Plus.
```

Example 29

Printed side of compact disk

Example 29

```
HyperCard stacks [computer file] / Educorp. -- Version 3.0. -- San
    Diego, CA : Educorp Computer Services, c1990.
        1 computer disk ; 4 3/4 in.

        System requirements: Macintosh; CD-ROM drive.
        Title from disk label.
        Summary: Contains stackware of all types from Educorp's
    library of public domain and shareware software.


        1. Hyper Card (Computer program)  I. Educorp Computer
    Services.  II. Title: Educorp hypercard stacks.  III.
    Macintosh.

        QA76.6.H8
```

I used "Educorp" as a statement of responsiblity because of the layout of information on the disk label. It might also be considered to be the first word of the title, so I made a title added entry for the alternate form.

No printed material came with this. The description is based on information in the Educorp catalog.

Rules for notes are 9.7B1b, 9.7B3, 9.7B17.

```
Type: m       Bib lvl: m Source: d    Lang: eng
File: m       Enc lvl: I Govt pub:    Ctry: cau
Audience: f Mod rec:     Frequen: n  Regulr:
Desc: a       Dat tp: s  Dates: 1990,
 1 010
 2 040        XXX ǂc XXX
 3 090        QA76.6.H8
 4 049        XXXX
 5 245 00     HyperCard stacks ǂh computer file  / ǂc Educorp
 6 250        Version 3.0
 7 260        San Diego, CA : ǂb Educorp Computer Services, ǂc c1990.
 8 300        1 computer disk ; ǂc 4 3/4 in.
 9 538        System requirements: Macintosh; CD-ROM drive.
10 500        Title from disk label.
11 520        Contains stackware of all types from Educorp's library of public
domain and shareware software.
12 630 00     HyperCard (Computer program)
13 710 20     Educorp Computer Services.
14 740 01     Educorp hypercard stacks.
15 753        Macintosh.
```

94

Example 30

Printed side of
compact disk

Cover of guide

Example 30

```
Desert storm [computer file] : the war in the Persian Gulf / a
    product of Warner New Media in association with Time magazine.
    -- Burbank, CA : Warner New Media, c1991.
    1 computer disk : sd., col. ; 4 3/4 in. + 1 guide.

    System requirements: Macintosh Plus or higher; 2MB RAM;
    System 6.0.5 or higher; Apple-compatible SCSI CD-ROM drive.
    Title from disk label.
    Summary: Multimedia disc includes correspondents' reports,
    eyewitness accounts, photos, sound recordings, maps, charts,
    research, and key documents gathered by the editorial staff of
    Time during the Gulf War.


    1. Persian Gulf War, 1991.  2. United States--History,
    Military--20th century.  3. Persian Gulf Region--History.  4.
    Iraq--History--1958-      I. Warner New Media.  II. Macintosh
    Plus.

    DS79.72
```

This multimedia item is described here as a computer disk, though its contents are similar to those of many video discs. Guidelines for cataloging interactive multimedia material are being developed.

I coded "Audience" as "g" for general for this item
We can code the time period covered in field 045.
Rules for notes are 9.7B1b, 9.7B3, 9.7B7.

```
Type: m      Bib lvl: m Source: d   Lang: eng
File: m      Enc lvl: I Govt pub:   Ctry: cau
Audience: g Mod rec:   Frequen: n  Regulr:
Desc: a      Dat tp: s  Dates: 1991,
 1 010
 2 040     XXX ǂc XXX
 3 043
 4 045 2   ǂb d19907 ǂb d19913
 5 090     DS79.72
 6 245 00 Desert Storm ǂh computer file : ǂb the war in the Persian Gulf / ǂc a
product of Warner New Media in association with Time magazine.
 7 260     Burbank, CA : ǂb Warner New Media, ǂc c1991.
 8 300     1 computer disk : ǂb sd., col. ; ǂc 4 3/4 in. ǂe + 1 guide.
 9 538     System requirements: Macintosh Plus or higher; 2MB RAM; System 6.0.5
or higher; Apple-compatible SCSI CD-ROM drive.
10 500     Title from disk label.
11 520     Multimedia disc includes correspondents' reports, eyewitness
accounts, photos, sound recordings, maps, charts, research, and key documents
gathered by the editorial staff of Time during the Gulf War.
12 651  0 Persian Gulf War, 1991.
13 651  0 United States ǂx History, Military ǂy 20th century
14 651  0 Persian Gulf Region ǂx History.
15 740 01 Iraq ǂx History ǂy 1958-
16 710 20 Warner New Media.
17 753     Macintosh Plus.
```

96

Example 31

Box cover

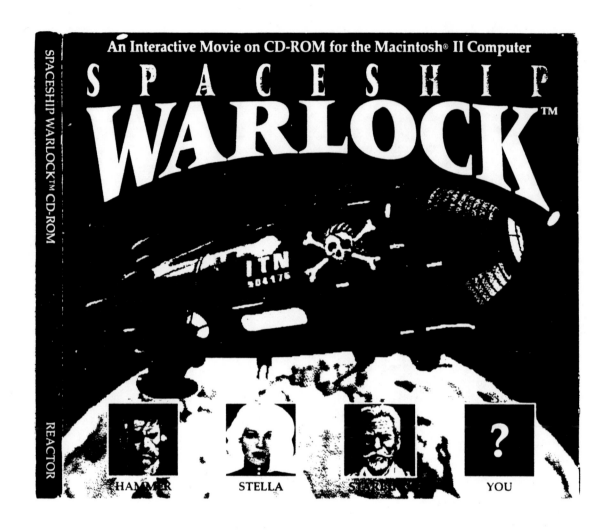

Example 31

Box cover

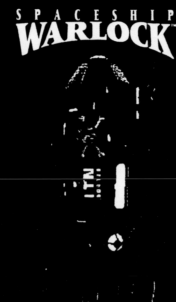

TRAILBLAZING COMPUTER ENTERTAINMENT!

SPACESHIP
WARLOCK™

REACTOR

MIKE SAENZ
Director, Writer, Artist,
Animator and Programmer
on Spaceship Warlock.

A former comic book
artist/writer for Marvel
Comics and a computer
entertainment pioneer,
Saenz brings his
trailblazing vision,
storytelling talents and
distinctive visual style to
Spaceship Warlock.

JOE SPARKS
3D Artist, Animator,
Musician and Programmer
on Spaceship Warlock.

A former aerospace
simulation artist for
Nasa/Ames Research
and an acclaimed
musician, Sparks makes
his auspicious debut in
the computer
entertainment industry
with Spaceship Warlock.

SPACESHIP WARLOCK™ CD-ROM

ABOUT REACTOR

**Reactor is a developer and publisher of innovative interactive entertainment
products on CD-ROM. Send in your registration card today to ensure that you'll
stay notified of new releases and product updates!**

98

Example 31

CD label
[The word "Spaceship"
appears above the word
"Warlock"]

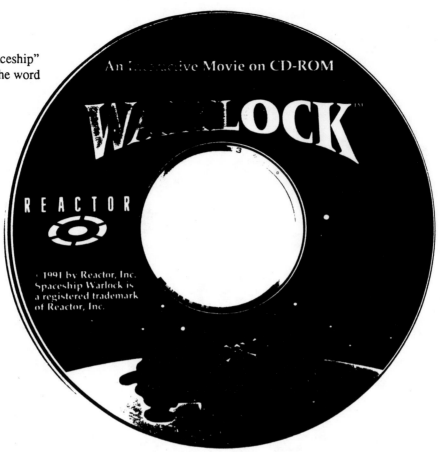

Saenz, Mike.
     Spaceship Warlock [computer file] / [Mike Saenz, Joe Sparks].
-- [United States] : Reactor, c1991.
     1 computer disk : sd., col. ; 4 3/4 in.

     "An interactive movie on CD-ROM for the Macintosh II computer"
--Container.
     System requirements: Macintosh II or greater; 4 MB RAM; CD-ROM
drive, 13 in. or larger color monitor.
     Title from disk label.
     Summary: "You are aboard the Spaceliner Belshazzar out of
Stambul when the pirate ship Warlock attacks. The dark ship shrugs
off the Belshazzar's heaviest weapons and the marauders pour
through the hull. Captured and taken aboard the pirate vessel, you
are about to embark on a journey beyond imagining, a journey
across the galaxy in the ultimate adventure"--Container.

     1. Computer adventure games. I. Sparks, Joe. II. Reactor,
Inc. III. Title. IV. Macintosh II (Computer).

GV1469.22

(Continued on next page)

Example 31

I bracketed the names of the two people into the statement of responsibility because they were so prominently named and pictured on the container. They each performed multiple functions in the creation of this game; I chose not to list those functions.

The country is coded as "xxu" for United States.

Rules for notes are 9.7B1a, 9.7B1b, 9.7B3, 9.7B17.

```
Type: m       Bib lvl: m Source: d    Lang: eng
File: m       Enc lvl: I Govt pub:    Ctry: xxu
Audience: g Mod rec:     Frequen: n   Regulr:
Desc: a       Dat tp: s  Dates: 1991,
 1 010
 2 040      XXX ‡c XXX
 3 090      GV1469.22
 4 049      XXXX
 5 100 1    Saenz, Mike.
 6 245 10   Spaceship Warlock ‡h computer file / ‡c [Mike Saenz, Joe Sparks]
 7 260      [United States] : ‡b Reactor, ‡c c1991.
 8 300      1 computer disk : ‡b sd., col. ; ‡c 3 1/2 in.
 9 500      "An interactive movie on CD-ROM for the Macintosh II computer"--
Container.
10 538      System requirements: Macintosh II or greater; 4 MB RAM; CD-ROM drive;
13 in. or larger color monitor.
11 500      Title from disk label.
12 520      "You are aboard the Spaceliner Belshazzar out of Stambul when the
pirate ship Warlock attacks. The dark ship shrugs off the Belshazzar's heaviest
weapons and the marauders pour through the hull. Captured and taken abouard the
pirate vessel, you are about to embark on a journey beyond imagining, a journey
across the galaxy in the ultimate adventure"--Container.
13 650  0   Computer adventure games.
14 700 10   Sparks, Joe.
15 710 20   Reactor, Inc.
16 753      Macintosh II (Computer).
```

100

Example 32

Box label

In Apple® Sound
Resource Format

Sound FX
Volume 1

CD label

In Apple®Sound
Resource Format

Sound FX
Volume 1

REFLECTIVE ARTS
INTERNATIONAL

Example 32

```
Desktop sounds [computer file]. -- [United States] : Reflective
   Arts International, 1989-
        computer disks : sd. ; 4 3/4 in.

     Digital sound effects for the Macintosh.
     System requirements: Macintosh Plus, SE, or II; System and
   Finder version 6.0.2 or higher; HyperCard version 1.2.2 or
   higher; Apple CD SC or compatible CD-ROM drive.
     Title from disk label.
     Copyright by Optical Media International.
     Partial contents: Vol. 1. Sound FX.


     1. Sounds.  2. Macintosh (Computer)--Sound effects.  I.
   Reflective Arts International.  II. Optical Media
   International.  III. Macintosh Plus.

   QA76.9.S6
```

This is cataloged as an open entry because the disk is labeled as volume 1. It is not a serial because we can assume an end is planned. The ending date of publication for this set is not known. A partial contents note is used.

Rules for notes are 9.7B1a, 9.7B1b, 9.7B3, 9.7B6, 9.7B18.

```
Type: m       Bib lvl: m Source: d    Lang: eng
File: m       Enc lvl: I Govt pub:    Ctry: xxu
Audience: f Mod rec:    Frequen: n  Regulr:
Desc: a       Dat tp: m  Dates: 1989,9999
 1 010
 2 040     XXX ǂc XXX
 3 090     QA76.9.S6
 4 049     XXXX
 5 245 00  Desktop sounds ǂh computer file
 6 260     [United States] : ǂb Reflective Arts International, ǂc 1989-
 7 300         computer disks : ǂb sd. ; ǂc 4 3/4 in.
 8 538     System requirements: Macintosh Plus, SE, or II; System and Finder
version 6.0.2 or higher; Hyper Card version 1.2.2 or higher; Apple CD SC or
compatible CD-ROM drive.
 9 500     Title from disk label.
10 500     Copyright by Optical Media International.
11 505 2   Vol. 1. Sound FX.
12 650  0  Sounds.
13 630 00  Macintosh (Computer) ǂx Sound effects.
14 710 20  Reflective Arts International.
15 710 20  Optical Media International.
16 753     Macintosh Plus.
```

Example 33A (monograph)

CD container label

You are holding the world's first fully integrated multimedia magazine. It combines text, sound, graphics, animations, talking agents, video and music — all at your command through an engaging point and click interface. VERBUM INTERACTIVE 1.0 was developed by *Verbum* magazine, the cutting edge of digital art and design since 1986. This inaugural edition of VI is already a collector's item!

The Verbum Roundtable interactive panel discussion with six multimedia industry leaders, including text, audio and video clips.

The digital avant-garde: the VI Gallery of animation and interactive multimedia.

Interactive Feature Stories
"Interactive Marketing by Design" by Hal Josephson — including outstanding sample applications.
"Global Media and Common Ground" by Brenda Laurel — an extended essay (for printing) and a stunning audio/visual annotation.
"New Media and the Macintosh in Advertising" by Jennifer Omholt – a survey with samples of multimedia presentations by top agencies.
"Creative Cyberculture" by Michael Gosney – a review of key events in the digital art world, with video clips.
"Multimedia in Education" by Linnea Dayton — with excerpts from an interview with Bill Atkinson and sample educational programs.

The Verbum How-To
"Painted Faces — Type Effects with Photoshop" by Jack Davis – a step-by-step program tutorial.

Demo Programs, Files and Product Tutorials

Verbum Music
These stereo tracks (only *some* of the music on VI) will play in any audio CD player.
① (Skip this track – computer data)
② Spy Cruisin' – Geno Andrews
③ Davis Jam – Geno Andrews
④ Dance – D'Cückoo
⑤ Gaya's Eyes* (part) – Todd Rundgren
⑥ Travelling Rogue – Christopher Yavelow
⑦ Listening for Life – Pauline Oliveros
⑧ Wind on the Water** (part) – Crosby, Stills and Nash

PUBLISHED BY VERBUM, INC.
PO BOX 12564, SAN DIEGO, CA 92112
$49.95   VI 1.0

MACINTOSH EDITION / Required system configuration: Color Macintosh with 5 MB RAM, 13-inch monitor (or larger) and CD-ROM player.
Entire contents copyright © 1991 by VERBUM, Inc., with the exception of paid demo files and editorial sample files, which are copyrighted by their respective owners.
* Courtesy Warner Brothers Records, Inc .from the album "2nd Wind"   **Courtesy MCA Records and Graham Nash, from the album "Wind on the Water"

Example 33A (monograph)

```
Verbum interactive. Issue 1.0 [computer file]. -- Macintosh ed. --
   San Deigo, CA : Verbum, c1991.
      2 computer disks : sd., col. ; 4 3/4 in.

      Inaugural ed. of CD-ROM multimedia magazine.
      System requirements: Macintosh; 5MB RAM; CD-ROM player; 13-
   inch color monitor or larger.
      Title from container.
      Contents: Verbum round table [3 hr. panel discussion on the
   multimedia field] -- Digital avant-garde [animation and
   interactive multimedia] -- Interactive feature stories [5
   items] -- The Verbum how-to [animated tutorial on type effects]
   -- Demo programs, files, and product tutorials -- Verbum music
   [7 stereo tracks].


      1. Interactive television.  I. Verbum, Inc.  II. Macintosh.

   QA76.9.I57
```

This is cataloged both as a monograph and as a serial. The monographic record gives some indication of contents for the two disks, although the amount of material that can be contained on two CD-ROM disks is so great that these contents notes cannot be too specific.

Rules for notes are (monograph) 9.7B1a, 9.7B1b, 9.7B3, 9.7B18; (serial) 9.7B1a, 9.7B1b, 9.7B3.

```
Type: m      Bib lvl: m Source: d   Lang: eng
File: m      Enc lvl: I Govt pub:   Ctry: cau
Audience: f Mod rec:    Frequen: n  Regulr:
Desc: a      Dat tp: s  Dates: 1991,
 1 010
 2 040       XXX ǂc XXX
 3 090       QA76.9.I57
 4 049       XXXX
 5 245 00    Verbum interactive. ǂn Issue 1.0 ǂh computer file
 6 250       Macintosh ed.
 7 260       San Diego, CA : ǂb Verbum, ǂc c1991.
 8 300       2 computer disks ; ǂb sd., col. ; ǂc 4 3/4 in.
 9 500       Inaugural ed. of CD-ROM multimedia magazine.
10 538       System requirements: Macintosh; 5MB RAM; CD-ROM player; 13-inch color
monitor or larger.
11 500       Title from container.
12 505 0     Verbum round table [3 hr. panel discussion on the multimedia field]
-- Digital avant-garde [animation and interactive multimedia] -- Interactive
feature stories [5 items] -- The Verbum how-to [animated tutorial on type
effects] -- Demo programs, files, and product tutorials -- Verbum music [7
stereo tracks].
13 650  0    Interactive television.
14 710 20    Verbum, Inc.
15 753       Macintosh,
```

104

Example 33B (serial)

```
Verbum interactive [computer file]. -- Macintosh ed. -- Issue 1.0-
      . -- San Diego, CA : Verbum, c1991-
         computer disks : sd., col. ; 4 3/4 in.

      CD-ROM multimedia magazine.
      System requirements: Macintosh; 5MB RAM; CD-ROM player; 13-
   inch color monitor or larger.
      Title from container.


      1. Interactive television--Periodicals.  I. Verbum, Inc.
   II. Macintosh.

      QA76.9.I57
```

The frequency of this item is unknown.


```
Type: m      Bib lvl: s Source: d    Lang: eng
File: m      Enc lvl: I Govt pub:    Ctry: cau
Audience: f Mod rec:    Frequen: u  Regulr: u
Desc: a      Pub st: c  Dates: 1991-9999
 1 010
 2 040      XXX ǂc XXX
 3 090      QA76.9.I57
 4 049      XXXX
 5 245 00   Verbum interactive ǂh computer file
 6 250      Macintosh ed.
 7 362 0    Issue 1.0-
 8 260      San Diego, CA : ǂb Verbum, ǂc c1991-
 9 300         computer disks : ǂb sd., col. ; ǂc 4 3/4 in.
10 500      CD-ROM multimedia magazine.
11 538      System requirements: Macintosh; 5 MB RAM; CD-ROM player; 13-inch
color monitor or larger.
12 500      Title from container.
13 650   0  Interactive television ǂx Periodicals.
14 710 20 Verbum, Inc.
15 753      Macintosh.
```

Example 34A

Computer disk

From cover of guide

```
National Gallery of Art [computer file] : a videodisc companion --
   Santa Monica, Calif. : The Voyager Company, c1991.
      1 computer disk ; 3 1/2 in. + 1 guide.

      System requirements: Macintosh Plus, Macintosh SE, or
   Macintosh II with hard disk drive; videodisc player with an RS-
   232 interface; HyperCard 2.0; National Gallery of Art
   videodisc.
      Title from disk label.
      Summary: Designed as index for: The National Gallery of Art.
   Allows easy organization and viewing in such categories as
   artist, nationality, period/style, date, medium, and subject.
```

(Continued on next page)

Example 34A

> 1. National Gallery of Art (Videorecording)--Indexes. 2.
> National Gallery of Art (U.S.)--History--Indexes. 3. National
> Gallery of Art (U.S.)--Catalogs and collections--Indexes. 4.
> Art--History--Indexes. 5. Painting--Wshington (D.C.)--Indexes.
> 6. Sculpture--Washington (D.C)--Indexes. 7. Drawing--
> Washington (D.C.)--Indexes. 8. Art museums--Washington (D.C.)
> --Indexes. I. Voyager Company. II. Macintosh Plus. III.
> Macintosh SE. IV. Macintosh II.

> N856

This disk is to be used with a videodisc published earlier by another agency. The cataloging for the videodisc is shown following this example. The combination is interactive, allowing random access, searching in various ways, and retrieval of information for creation of various products.

Rules for notes are: 9.7B1b, 9.7B3, 9.7B17.

```
Type: m      Bib lvl: m Source: d   Lang: eng
File: b      Enc lvl: I Govt pub:   Ctry: cau
Audience: f Mod rec:    Frequen: n  Regulr:
Desc: a      Dat tp: s  Dates: 1991,
 1 010
 2 040     XXX ǂc XXX
 3 090     N856
 4 049     XXXX
 5 245 00  National Gallery of Art ǂh computer file : ǂb a videodisc companion.
 6 260     Santa Monica, Calif. : ǂb The Voyager Company, ǂc c1991.
 7 300     1 computer disk ; ǂc 3 1/2 in. + ǂe 1 guide.
 8 538     System requirements: Macintosh Plus, Macintosh SE, or Macintosh II
with hard disk drive; videodisc player with an RS-232 interface; HyperCard 2.0;
National Gallery of Art videodisc.
 9 500     Title from disk label.
10 520     Designed as index for: The National Gallery of Art. Allows easy
organization and viewing in such categories as artist, nationality, period/
style, date, medium, and subject.
11 630 00  National Gallery of Art (Videorecording) ǂx Indexes.
12 610 21  National Gallery of Art (U.S.) ǂx History ǂx Indexes.
13 610 20  National Gallery of Art (U.S.) ǂx Catalogs and collections ǂx
Indexes.
14 650  0  Art ǂx History ǂx Indexes.
15 650  0  Painting ǂz Washington (D.C.) ǂx Indexes.
16 650  0  Sculpture ǂz Washington (D.C.) ǂx Indexes.
17 650  0  Drawing ǂz Washington (D.C.) ǂx Indexes.
18 650  0  Art museums ǂz Washington (D.C.) ǂx Indexes.
19 710 20  Voyager Company.
20 753     Macintosh Plus.
21 753     Macintosh SE.
22 753     Macintosh II.
```

Example 34B

Videodisc labels

108

Example 34B

From disc jacket

Manufactured by Pioneer Video, Inc. by license under several pending patents.

STANDARD PLAY (CAV format). You can utilize freeze frame, slow motion, random access, 3 x fast, and scan on this disc.

Warning: All rights reserved. Unauthorized public performance, broadcasting or copying is a violation of applicable laws. This motion picture is protected under laws of the United States and other countries. Unauthorized duplication, distrubution or exhibition may result in civil liability and criminal prosecution. Copyright 1983 Videodisc Publishing, Inc. 381 Park Avenue South, Suite 1601, New York, New York 10016. When not in use, place videodisc in jacket and store in a cool, dry place.

 Stereo

VPI-NGA-84

```
National Gallery of Art (Videorecording)
     National Gallery of Art [videorecording] / Videodisc Pub-
lishing, Inc., and Vidmax ; written, directed, and produced by
Jerry Whiteley. -- New York, N.Y. : Ztek, c1983.
     1 videodisc : sd., col. ; 12 in. + 1 index (8 p. ; 31 cm.)

     Accompanying index lists frame numbers for painters and
their individual works.
     Laser optical, standard play CAV format; stereo.
     Side 1. The history of the National Gallery of Art (22 min.,
17 sec.) -- side 2. The videodisc catalogue / [producer, Anne
Marie Garti] (3353 fr.) [1645 works of art with descriptions].
A tour of the National Gallery of Art (27 min., 22 sec.).
     Narrator: J. Carter Brown.
     "VPI-NGA-84."


     1. National Gallery of Art (U.S.)--History.  2. National
Gallery of Art (U.S.)--Catalogs and collections.  3. Art--
History.  4. Painting--Washington, (D.C.)  5. Sculpture--
Washington (D.C.)  6. Drawing--Washington, (D.C.)  7. Art
museums--Washington (D.C.)  I. Whiteley, Jerry.  II. Garti,
Anne Marie.  III. Brown, J. Carter (John Carter), 1934-    .
IV. National Gallery of Art (U.S.)  V. Videodisc Publishing,
Inc.  VI. Ztek (Firm)
```

Example 34B

```
Type: g      Bib lvl: m Source: d  Lang: eng
Type mat: v Enc lvl: I Govt pub:   Ctry: nyu
Int lvl: g  Mod rec:   Tech: l     Leng:
Desc: a      Accomp: s  Dat tp: s  Dates: 1983,
 1 010
 2 040      ‡c MNM
 3 007      ‡v b ‡f d ‡c e ‡g f ‡a g ‡i h ‡z
 4 090      ‡b
 5 130 0    National Gallery of Art (Videorecording)
 6 245 00   National Gallery of Art ‡h videorecording / ‡c Videodisc Publishing,
Inc., and Vidmax ; written, directed, and produced by Jerry Whiteley.
 7 260      New York, N.Y. : ‡b Ztek, ‡c c1983.
 8 300      1 videodisc : ‡b sd., col. ; ‡c 12 in. + ‡e 1 index (8 p. ; 31 cm.)
 9 500      Accompanying index lists frame numbers for painters and their
individual works.
10 500      Laser optical, standard play CAV format; stereo.
11 505 0    Side 1. The history of the National Gallery of Art (22 min., 17 sec.)
-- side 2. The videodisc catalogue / [producer, Anne Marie Garti] (3353 fr. )
[1645 works of art with descriptions]. A tour of the National Gallery of Art (27
min., 22 sec.).
12 511 3    J. Carter Brown.
13 500      "VPI-NGA-84."
14 610 20   National Gallery of Art (U.S.) ‡x History.
15 610 20   National Gallery of Art (U.S.) ‡x Catalogs and collections.
16 650  0   Art ‡x History.
17 650  0   Painting ‡z Washington, (D.C.)
18 650  0   Sculpture ‡z Washington (D.C.)
19 650  0   Drawing ‡z Washington (D.C.)
20 650  0   Art museums ‡z Washington (D.C.)
21 700 10   Whiteley, Jerry.
22 700 10   Garti, Anne Marie.
23 700 10   Brown, J. Carter ‡q (John Carter), ‡d 1934-
24 710 20   National Gallery of Art (U.S.)
25 710 20   Videodisc Publishing, Inc.
26 710 20   Ztek (Firm)
```

Example 35

Compact disc label

```
1987 economic censuses [computer file] : report series. --
    Washington DC : U.S. Dept. of Commerce, Bureau of the Census,
    Data User Services Division, [1989-
         computer disks ; 4 3/4 in. +    computer disks +    sets
    of technical documentation.

         System requirements: IBM PC, XT, AT, or compatible; 640K;
    MS-DOS 3.1 or higher; CD-ROM Extensions (2.0 or higher); CD-ROM
    drive.
         Title from title screen.
         Files contain statistical data on retail trade, wholesale
    trade, service industries, transportation, and manufactures.
         Will be published in two volumes; cumulative releases issued
    as data becomes available.


         1. United States--Industries--Statistics.  2. United States
    --Economic conditions--1981-     --Statistics.  I. United
    States. Bureau of the Census. Data User Services Division.  II.
    Economic censuses.  III. IBM PC.

    HA201 1987
```

Example 35

This CD-ROM is not a serial, as it will be complete in two volumes.

In these examples, I have treated the program disks as accompanying material with the CD-ROM data disks as the main item.

"File" is coded "a" for numeric data.

It is a government publication, so is coded "f" for federal government publication.

Rules for notes are: 9.7B1b, 9.7B3, 9.7B8, 9.7B9.

```
Type: m       Bib lvl: m Source: d    Lang: eng
File: a       Enc lvl: I Govt pub: f Ctry: dcu
Audience: f Mod rec:    Frequen: n  Regulr:
Desc: a       Dat tp: m  Dates: 1989, 9999
 1 040      XXX ǂc XXX
 2 074      154-C
 3 086 0    C 3.277:Ec 7/987/CD/v.1 rel.1 A-
 4 090      HA201 ǂb 1987
 5 049      XXXX
 6 245 00   1987 economic censuses ǂh computer file : ǂb report series.
 7 260      Washington, DC : ǂb U.S. Dept. of Commerce, Bureau of the Census,
Data User Services Division, ǂc 1989-
 8 300         computer disks ; ǂc 4 3/4 in. + ǂe    computer disks +    sets of
technical documentation.
 9 538      System requirements: IBM-PC, XT, AT or compatible; MS-DOS 3.1 or
higher; CD-ROM Extensions (2.0 or higher); CD-ROM drive.
10 500      Title from title screen.
11 500      Files contain statistical data on retail trade, wholesale trade,
service industries, transportation, and manufactures.
12 500      Will be published in two volumes; cumulative releases issued as data
becomes available.
13 651  0   United States ǂx Industries ǂx Statistics
14 651  0   United States ǂx Economic conditions ǂy 1981- ǂx Statistics.
15 710 10   United States. ǂb Bureau of the Census. ǂb Data User Services
Division.
16 740 01   Economic censuses.
17 753      IBM PC.
```

Example 36

CD label

U.S. exports of merchandise [computer file]. -- Washington, DC :
   U.S. Dept. of Commerce, Bureau of the Census, Data User
   Services Division,
        computer disks ; 4 3/4 in. + 1 computer disk (5 1/4 in.)
   + 1 set of technical documentation.

   Monthly.
   Description based on: June 1991.
   System requirements: IBM PC, XT, AT, or compatible; CD-ROM
drive.
   Title from disk label.
   Title of 5 1/4 in. disk reads: Exports—for monthly export
data. Title on technical documentation: U.S. exports and
imports of merchandise on CD-ROM, technical documentation.
   Began with Sept. 1989.
   Each issue supersedes previous issue.
   Some vols. issued by: Foreign Trade Division.
   ISSN 1057-8773 = U.S. exports of merchandise.

(Continued on next page)

Example 36

```
        1. Commercial products--United States--Statistics--
Information services.  2. Exports--United States--Statistics--
Information services.  3. United States--Commerce--Statistics--
Information services.  I. United States. Bureau of the Census.
Data User Services Division.  II. United States. Bureau of the
Census. Foreign Trade Division.  III. U.S. exports and imports
of merchandise on CD-ROM, technical documentation.  IV. Title:
Exports—for monthly export data.  V. IBM PC.


HF3000
```

Examples 36 to 40 are cataloged as serials even though the disks are cumulative with various replacement patterns. This type of material is being published in an increasing number of titles for use in reference.
Rules for notes are: 12.7B1, 9.7B1b, 9.7B3, 9.7B4, 12.7B8, 12.7B9, 12.7B9, 12.7B23.

```
Type: m       Bib lvl: m Source: d    Lang: eng
File: a       Enc lvl: I Govt pub: f Ctry: dcu
Audience: f Mod rec:    Frequen: m  Regulr: r
Desc: a       Pub st: c  Dates: 1990-9999
 1 040      XXX ‡c XXX
 2 022      1057-8773
 3 086 0    C 3.278:Ex 7/
 4 090      HF3000
 5 049      XXXX
 6 222  0   U.S. exports of merchandise
 7 245 00   U.S. exports of merchandise ‡h computer file
 8 260      Washington, DC : ‡b U.S. Dept. of Commerce, Bureau of the Census,
Data User Services Division,
 9 300          computer disks ; ‡c 4 3/4 in. + ‡e 1 computer disk (5 1/4 in.) +
1 set of technical documentation.
10 315      Monthly.
11 500      Description based on: June 1991.
12 538      System requirements: IBM-PC, AT, XT, or compatible CD-ROM drive.
13 500      Title from disk label.
14 500      Title of 5 1/4 in. disk reads: Exports—for monthly export data. Title
on technical documentation: U.S. exports and imports of merchandise on CD-ROM,
technical documentation.
15 362 1    Began with Sept. 1989.
16 500      Each issue supersedes previous issue.
17 500      Some vols. issued by: Foreign Trade Division.
18 650  0   Commercial products ‡z United States ‡x Statistics ‡x Information
services.
19 650  0   Exports ‡z United States ‡x Statistics ‡x Information serives.
20 651  0   United States ‡x Commerce ‡x Statistics ‡x Information services.
21 710 10   United States. ‡b Bureau of the Census. ‡b Data User Services
Division.
22 710 10   United States. ‡b Bureau of the Census. ‡b Foreign Trade Division.
23 730 01   U.S. exports and imports of merchandise on CD ROM, technical
documentation.
24 740 01   Exports—for monthly export data.
25 753      IBM PC.
```

114

Example 37

CD label

Example 37

The National trade data bank [computer file] : NTDB. -- Oct. 1990-
. -- [Washington, D.C.] : U.S. Dept. of Commerce, Economics
and Statistics Administration, Office of Business Analysis,
[1990-
computer disks ; 4 3/4 in.

Monthly.
System requirements: IBM XT, AT, 386, PS/2 or compatible;
512K; Microsoft CD-ROM extensions installed under PC or MS-DOS
(V3.1 or later version); CD-ROM drive; hard disk.
Title from disk label.
Manual may be printed from disk or obtained from NTIS.

1. Exports--United States--Statistics--Periodicals. 2.
United States--Commerce--Statistics--Periodicals. I. United
States. Bureau of the Census. Office of Business Analysis. II.
Title: NTDB. III. IBM XT.

HF1414.4

Rules for notes are: 12.7B1, 9.7B1b, 9.7B3, 12.7B8, 9.7B11.

Type: m   Bib lvl: s Source: d   Lang: eng
File: a   Enc lvl: I Govt pub: f Ctry: dcu
Audience: f Mod rec: Frequen: m Regulr: r
Desc: a   Pub st: c Dates: 1990-9999
 1 040   XXX ‡c XXX
 3 086 0   C 1.88:
 4 090   HF1414.4
 5 049   XXXX
 6 245 04   The National trade data bank ‡h computer file : ‡b NTDB.
 7 260   [Washington, D.C.] : ‡b U.S. Dept. of Commerce, Economics and
Statistics Administration, Office of Business Analysis, ‡c [1990-
 8 300   computer disks ; ‡c 4 3/4 in.
 9 315   Monthly.
10 362 0   Oct. 1990-
11 538   System requirements: IBM XT, AT, 386, PS/2 or compatible; 512K;
Microsoft CD-ROM extensive installed under PC or MS-DOS (V3.1 or later version);
CD-ROM drive; hard disk.
12 500   Title from disk label.
13 650 0 Exports ‡z United States ‡x Statistics ‡x Periodicals.
14 651 0 United States ‡x Commerce ‡x Statistics ‡x Periodicals.
15 710 10 United States. ‡b Bureau of the Census. ‡b Office of Business
Analysis.
16 740 01 NTDB.
17 753   IBM XT.

Example 38

CD label

Corporate information on public companies filing with the SEC
    [computer file] : including Disclosure spectrum. --   . --
Bethesda, MD : Disclosure, 1990-
        computer disks ; 4 3/4 in. + 1 computer disk (5 1/4 in.)
+ 1 user's manual.

    Quarterly.
    Description based on: Aug. 1990.
    System requirements: IBM PC, XT or AT, PS/2 or compatible;
640K with 2.5 MB on hard disk; CD-ROM drive; printer.
    Title from disk label.
    Summary: Disclosure database contains financial and
management information on over 12,000 public companies.
Spectrum ownership database contains detailed tables with
institutional, five percent, and insider stock owners. Zacks
earnings estimate database includes research and analysis from
more than 120 brokerage houses. Allows data to be downloaded
for personal use.

    1. Corporations--United States--Statistics--Periodicals. I.
Disclosure (Firm) II. IBM PC.

HD2741

Example 38

Rules for notes are 12.7B1, 9.7B1b, 9.7B3, 9.7B17.

```
Type: m      Bib lvl: s Source: d   Lang: eng
File: m      Enc lvl: I Govt pub: f Ctry: mdu
Audience: f Mod rec:   Frequen: q  Regulr: r
Desc: a      Pub st: c Dates: 1990-9999
 1 040      XXX ǂc XXX
 2 090      HD2741
 3 049      XXXX
 4 245 00  Corporate information on public companies filing with the SEC ǂh
computer file : ǂb including Disclosure spectrum.
 5 260      Bethesda, MD : ǂb Disclosure, ǂc 1990-
 6 300         computer disks ; ǂc 4 3/4 in. + ǂe 1 computer disk (5 1/4 in.) + 1
user's manual.
 7 315      Quarterly.
 8 500      Description based on: Aug. 1990.
 9 538      System requirements: IBM PC, XT or AT, PS/2, or compatible; 640K with
2.5 MB on hard disk; CD-ROM drive; printer.
10 500      Title from disk label.
11 500      Disclosure database contains financial and management information on
over 12,000 public companies. Spectrum ownership database contains detailed
tables with institutional, five percent, and insider stock owners. Zacks
earnings estimate database includes research and analysis from more than 120
brokerage houses. Allows data to be downloaded for personal use.
12 650  0 Corporations ǂz United States ǂx Statistics ǂx Periodicals.
13 710 21 Disclosure (Firm)
14 710 10  IBM PC
```

118

Example 39

CD label

Example 39

```
PsycLIT [computer file] -- Boston, MA : SilverPlatter.
      computer disks ; 4 3/4 in. +    computer disk (5 1/4 in.)
   + 1 template + 1 manual.

      Quarterly.
      Description based on: SP-001-005 (1981-1986).
      System requirements: IBM PC, XT, AT or compatible; 512K; PC
   or MS DOS 2.1 or higher; hard disk drive, compact disc drive;
   printer.
      Title from disk label.
      1974-1982-
      Quarterly disks are cumulative. Basic disk covers 1974-1982.
      Summary: Summaries of the world's serial literature in
   psychology and related disciplines, compiled from the PsyINFO
   database produced by the American Psycholgical Association.


      1. Psychology--Abstracts.  2. Psychology--Periodicals.  I.
   SilverPlatter Information, Inc.  II. Title: Psyc Lit.  III. IBM
   PC.

      BF1
```

Rules for notes are: 12.7B1, 9.7B1b, 9.7B3, 12.7B8, 9.7B8, 9.7B17, 12.7B23.

```
Type: m      Bib lvl: s Source: d   Lang: eng
File: m      Enc lvl: I Govt pub:   Ctry: mau
Audience: f Mod rec:    Frequen: q  Regulr: r
Desc: a      Pub st: c  Dates: 1990-9999
 1 040     XXX ‡c XXX
 2 090     BF1
 3 049     XXXX
 4 245 00  PsycLIT ‡h computer file
 5 260     Boston, MA : ‡b SilverPlatter.
 6 300       computer disks ; ‡c 4 3/4 in. + ‡e   computer disks (5 1/4 in.) +
1 template + 1 manual.
 7 315     Quarterly.
 8 500     Description based on: SP-001-005 (1981-1986)
 9 538     System requirements: IBM PC, XT or AT or compatible; 512K; PC or MS
DOS 2.1 or higher; hard disk drive; compact disc drive; printer.
10 500     Title from disk label.
11 500     Quarterly disks are cumulative. Basic disk covers 1974-1982.
12 520     Summaries of the world's serial literature in psychology and related
disciplines, compiled from the PsyINFO database produced by the American
Psychological Association.
13 650  0  Psychology ‡x Abstracts.
14 650  0  Psychology ‡x Periodicals.
15 710 20  SilverPlatter Information, Inc.
16 740 01  Psyc Lit.
17 753     IBM PC.
```

120

Example 40A

CD label

ProQuest™

Periodical Abstracts

O N D I S C

Jan 1986-Dec 1988
Vol: **PA _ 86 _ 88**

U·M·I

Example 40A

> ProQuest periodical abstracts ondisc [computer file] -- Ann Arbor,
>   Mich. : UMI, 1989-
>   computer disks ; 4 3/4 in. + 1 computer disk (5 1/4 in.)
>   + 1 user's guide.
>
>   Monthly.
>   Description based on: Jan. 1986-Dec. 1988.
>   System requirements: IBM XT, AT or compatible, or IBM PS/2
> model 30; 640KB RAM; MS or PC DOS 2.0 or higher; hard disk
> drive, with at least 2MB disk space; CD-ROM drive; CD-ROM
> adapter card; monitor; printer optional.
>   Includes citations and abstracts to articles in over 300
> general/reference periodicals.
>
>
>   1. Periodicals--Indexes. 2. Periodicals--Abstracts--
> Indexes. I. University Microfilms International. II. Title:
> Periodical abstracts ondisc. III. Title: Periodical abstracts
> on disc. IV. IBM PC.
>
>   AI13

Rules for notes are: 12.7B1, 9.7B1b, 9.7B18.


```
Type: m      Bib lvl: s Source: d   Lang: eng
File: m      Enc lvl: I Govt pub:   Ctry: miu
Audience: f Mod rec:    Frequen: m  Regulr: r
Desc: a      Pub st: c  Dates: 1989-9999
 1 040    XXX +c XXX
 2 090    AI13
 3 049    XXXX
 4 245 00 ProQuest periodical abstracts ondisc +h computer file
 5 260    Ann Arbor, Mich. : +b UMI, +c 1989-
 6 300       computer disks ; +c 4 3/4 in. +e 1 computer disk (5 1/4 in.) + 1
user's guide.
 7 315    Monthly.
 8 500    Description based on: Jan. 1986-Dec. 1988.
 9 538    System requirements: IBM XT, AT or compatible, or IBM PS/2 model 30;
640KB RAM; MS or PC DOS 2.0 or higher; hard disk drive with at least 2MB disk
space; CD-ROM drive; CD-ROM adapter card; monitor; printer optional.
10 500    Includes citations and abstracts to articles in over 300 general/
reference periodicals.
11 650  0 Periodicals +x Indexes.
12 650  0 Periodicals +x Abstracts +x Indexes.
13 710 20 University Microfilms International.
14 740 01 Periodical abstracts ondisc.
15 740 01 Periodical abstracts on disc.
16 753    IBM PC.
```

Example 40B

CD label

ProQuest newspaper abstracts ondisc [computer file] -- Ann Arbor,
    Mich. : UMI,
        computer disks ; 4 3/4 in. + 1 installation disk + 1
user's guide + 1 thesaurus + 1 reference card + 1 template.

    Monthly, with biennial cumulations.
    Description based on Jan. 1990-Jan. 1991.
    System requirements: IBM XT, AT, or compatible, or IBM PS/2
model 30; 512KB RAM; MS or PC DOS 2.0 or higher; hard disk
drive with at least 2MB disk space; CD-ROM drive; printer
optional.
    Title from disk label.
    Summary: An electronic version of the printed UMI newspaper
indexes and the printed Wall Street journal index. Contains
abstracts of articles from the following newspapers: New York
times, Wall Street journal, Los Angeles times, Chicago tribune,
Christian Science monitor, Atlanta constitution/Atlanta
journal, Boston globe.

    1. Newspapers--Abstracts--Indexes. 2. Newspapers--Indexes.
I. University Microfilms Internaional. II. Title: Newspaper
abstracts ondisc. III. Title: Newspaper abstracts on disc.
IV. IBM PC.

AN1

Example 40B

Rules for notes are: 12.7B1, 9.7B1b, 9.7B3, 9.7B17, 12.7B23.

```
Type: m      Bib lvl: s Source: d   Lang: eng
File: m      Enc lvl: I Govt pub:   Ctry: miu
Audience: f Mod rec:   Frequen: m  Regulr: r
Desc: a      Pub st: c  Dates: 1990-9999
 1 040     XXX +c XXX
 2 090     AN1
 3 049     XXXX
 4 245 00  ProQuest newspaper abstracts ondisc +h computer file
 5 260     Ann Arbor, Mich. : +b UMI
 6 300        computer disks ; +c 4 3/4 in. +e 1 installation disk + 1 user's
guide + 1 thesaurus + 1 reference card + 1 template.
 7 315     Monthly, with biennial cumulations.
 8 500     Description based on Jan. 1990-Jan. 1991.
 9 538     System requirements: IBM XT, AT or compatible, or IBM PS/2 model 30;
512KB RAM; MS or PC DOS 2.0 or higher; hard disk drive with at lease 2MB disk
space; CD-ROM drive; printer optional.
10 500     Title from disk label.
11 520     An electronic version of the printed UMI newspaper indexes and the
printed Wall Street journal index. Contains abstracts of articles from the
following newspapers: New York times, Wall Street journal, Los Angeles times,
Chicago tribune, Christian Science monitor, Atlanta constitution/Atlanta
journal, Boston globe.
12 650  0  Newspapers +x Abstracts +x Indexes.
13 650  0  Newspapers +x Indexes.
14 710 20  University Microfilms International.
15 740 01  Newspaper abstracts ondisc.
16 740 01  Newspaper abstracts on disc.
17 753     IBM PC.
```